LIVERPOOL

Matthew Graham

HAMLYN

Cover photo is of Liverpool's lap of honour following their 1986 F.A. Cup and Double winning game against Everton.

The photograph on the endpapers is of Alan Kennedy's penalty which sealed victory in the 1984 European Cup for Liverpool in a penalty shoot-out, and the title-page photograph shows Liverpool players celebrating a previous victory in the competition, which the Reds have won four times.

Pages 10/11 *Three managers who in the 25 years between 1960 and 1984 changed Liverpool from a good Second Division side to the most successful club in Europe.*

LIVERPOOL

Contents

Photographic Acknowledgements
Cover photograph by Colorsport
Front cover inset by Allsport/David Cannon
All colour photographs by Peter Robinson and Allsport

Black and white photographs supplied by:
Allsport/Michael King
The Illustrated London News Picture Library
The Liverpool Daily Post and Echo
Peter Robinson

Published 1984 by
Hamlyn Publishing,
Bridge House, London Road,
Twickenham, Middlesex

Second revised edition 1986

ISBN 0 600 50339 9
Printed in Italy

The Early Days

Which Football League club first played at Anfield Road? And which other club from Liverpool started playing in blue shirts? The answers to these questions might surprise Liverpool Football Club supporters. It was Everton who first played at Anfield Road – and in red shirts at that. When Liverpool were set up as rivals, they played in blue.

Nowadays, of course, Liverpool are famous as the 'Super Reds', and Anfield, with its Kop and its knowledgeable supporters, is equally famous as the club's home. And the local rivals, Everton, are associated with the royal blue strip.

It all came about because of a dispute between a one-time Lord Mayor of Liverpool, John Houlding, and the Everton club of which he was a member and strong supporter. Everton had been formed in 1878 as St Domingo's Sunday School. They changed their name to Everton the next year and moved to Anfield in 1884, playing successively in salmon pink, black and scarlet, and ruby with dark blue facings. In 1888 they were founder members of the Football League, and the third League Champions in 1891. Houlding, a well-to-do local brewer who was known as 'King John of Everton', owned the site on which the Anfield Stadium was built. Everybody was happy.

It didn't last long. Houlding received rent from the club for the use of the ground, and this became the subject of a row. A majority of Everton members decided to move elsewhere and bought the ground which has now become Goodison Park. Houlding was stuck with his empty stadium, but being a man of resource he formed a new club and claimed that his new team was the real 'Everton'. Unfortunately the Football League and the Football Association did not agree with him. So Houlding had to find a new name for his team, and on 15 March 1892 Liverpool Football Club came into existence. The club colours were blue and white quarters.

The first Liverpool team to play in the Football League, in 1893-94, when the Second Division Championship was won.

The club immediately applied for membership of the Second Division, which was being formed that year. The application was turned down, so Liverpool played in the Lancashire League and won it. A new man took over at Liverpool, self-made businessman John McKenna. He applied again for membership of the Football League and this time Liverpool were accepted. So in their second season Liverpool were a League team – and they won the Second Division Championship, being unbeaten, winning 22 and drawing 6 of their 28 matches, with 77 goals against 18. They won by 8 points from Small Heath, later to become Birmingham City. In those days this did not guarantee promotion, the first three having to play the bottom three in the First Division in Test matches, the three winners going into the First Division next season. Liverpool played Newton Heath, later to become Manchester United, who had finished bottom in the First Division. Liverpool won 2-0, so in only their third season they were in the top flight.

Lincoln City had been the first League team to play Liverpool at Anfield, 5,000 spectators seeing Liverpool win 4-0. Now that they were in the First Division, Liverpool played the first two local derbies with Everton, who

John McKenna, the business man who took over Liverpool and gained entry into the Football League.

were one of the most successful sides in the country. Everton won 3-0 before 44,000 at Goodison Park and at Anfield 27,000 watched a 2-2 draw. The relative strengths of the teams were shown in the League table. Everton were second; Liverpool, in a close struggle with several other teams, finished last. They then lost their Test match with Second Division champions Bury 1-0, despite the Bury goalkeeper being sent off, and were relegated.

John McKenna's answer was to build – both on and off the field. A new stand was erected and new players signed. Liverpool had gone to Scotland for many of their early players – it was a period when Scotland was a major breeding ground of men who became Football League professionals. Indeed, Liverpool's team in their first League season must have caused some sort of record: although not all of them were Scots, eight of the team were – McOwen, McClean, McCartney, McCue, McBride, McVean, McQueen M and McQueen H. Now other Scots joined them, including George Allan, a fine international centre-forward who, sadly, was to die when only 24.

McKenna's boldness paid off – Liverpool topped the Second Division again. In 30 games they scored 106 goals, and won the championship on goal average from Manchester City. In this season, 1895-96, there were a series of eight Test matches, with the top two teams playing the bottom two of the First Division, home and away. Liverpool went up with five points from their four matches – City, however, stayed where they were with three points.

This time Liverpool established themselves in the top flight for a spell. They finished a good fifth (the first time they'd been higher than Everton) and reached the semi-final of the FA Cup before losing to Aston Villa, the strongest side in the country at the end of the last century, and who this season performed the double. It was a good year for Liverpool, who supplied two players to England, Harry Bradshaw and Frank Becton, as well as Allan to Scotland. And they made a decision which has significance even today – they changed their strip and wore for the first time the famous red shirts.

The Reds began to prosper and two seasons later (1898-99) they were in two great struggles, losing an FA Cup semi-final to Sheffield United 1-0 in the third replay and losing the Championship to Aston Villa in the last match of the season. The two teams were level on points, and met on the last day of the season. Villa had slightly the better goal average (the difference was of one goal), so Liverpool had to win. Alas, Villa rattled in a quick five goals and that was that.

Two years later, the first season of the twentieth century, it was Liverpool's turn. A 1-0 win on the last day of the season against bottom club West Brom gave Liverpool their first League Championship. The team was Perkins, Dunlop, Robertson T, Goldie, Raisbeck, Wilson, Fox, Satterthwaite, Raybould, Walker, Robertson J. The side was built round centre-half Alex Raisbeck, who was to play for Scotland for a number of years. In those days a centre-half was not a defender but the mid-field supporter of the attack, and Raisbeck was one of the original 'human dynamos'.

Liverpool could not shake off their alarming habit of being up one season and down the next, however, and three seasons later began a strange run. In 1903-04 they had dropped to next to bottom of the First Division, and since relegation was by now automatic, they started 1904-05 in the Second Division. Again new players were bought, and for the third time Liverpool won the Second Division Championship at the first attempt. They might go down, but they never stayed down.

Alex Raisbeck, the Scottish international centre-half, around whom the early teams of the twentieth century were built.

Opposite *Liverpool, dark shirts, play Sunderland, stripes, in 1896.*

The Match "Off-side"

Sunderland lodge a protest on account of bad light

First goal for Liverpool

17

The Reds' first season back was a great one for Merseyside. Liverpool took the Championship and Everton the FA Cup. The Liverpool side now included one of the great goalkeepers that have played for the club. Sam Hardy set the precedent. He was signed in 1905 from Chesterfield, and was England's regular goalkeeper from 1907 till 1920. The full team was: Hardy, Dunlop, West, Parry, Raisbeck, Bradley, Goddard, Robinson, Raybould, Carlin, Hewett. Joe Hewett was also helping to form a Liverpool tradition. He was one of those players who maintained a long-serving association with the Club after their playing days.

Liverpool now settled into a mid-table First Division side up to the First World War. The famous Kop, the huge covered slope behind one goal, was built, and named after Spion Kop, the hillside venue of a famous battle in the Boer War, where troops were packed so closely that machine guns caused wholesale slaughter. Jack Parkinson, a goal-scoring forward signed in the Second Division Championship year, was capped by England; Maurice Parry, George Lathom and Ernest Peake for Wales. Don McKinlay was signed in 1909 and played through to the end of the war, gaining Scottish caps. Bill Lacey, an international with Northern Ireland, was signed from Everton in 1912-13 and continued winning caps with Liverpool till 1922. He made a final appearance for his country in 1925, when playing with New Brighton. Sam Hardy was transferred to Aston Villa in 1912 and Bobby Campbell took over in goal.

In 1914 Liverpool reached the Cup Final for the first time. It was also the first time that Royalty attended – King George V was one of the guests of honour. The match was at Crystal Palace and the opponents were Burnley. London was invaded by Lancastrians, and nearly 73,000 attended. A brilliant goal by Freeman in the 58th minute – an unstoppable volley from a throw-in near the corner flag – won the match 1-0 for Burnley, but Liverpool pegged away, hit a post, and were a little unlucky to go down. The side was: Campbell, Longworth, Pursell, Fairfoul, Ferguson, McKinlay, Sheldon, Metcalfe, Miller, Lacey, Nicholl.

Meanwhile, the club's early chairman, John McKenna, had become one of the influential men in football's development (he was President of the Football League for 26 years). But Liverpool's last season before the war was marred by scandal. Eight players, five of whom were suspended, were found to be involved in fixing a match which the Reds lost to Manchester United 2-0 – the two points keeping Manchester United in the First Division.

After four years of war there were new faces in the side when football resumed in 1919. England internationals Tommy Bromilow and Harry Chambers were signed, but the biggest name in the side was Elisha Scott, a goalkeeper signed from Belfast Celtic in 1912. Scott played 429 matches for Liverpool and 31 for Northern Ireland. One of the all-time great goalkeepers, he was acknowledged as the best Ireland ever had until Pat Jennings came along to put in a challenge.

Liverpool began with greater consistency than before, and finished fourth in the first two post-war seasons. Then in 1921-22 they took their third Championship, with Scott conceding only 36 goals in 42 games. He did even better the following season, conceding only 31, and Liverpool won the Championship again. In both Championship seasons Liverpool won by six clear points. Stalwarts of the team were Scott, and his full-backs Longworth and McKinlay; Bromilow at half-back; Chambers, who scored 41 goals in the two seasons, and his wing partner Fred Hopkin, who scored only one – which coincided with a small fire in the Anfield grandstand, causing Hopkin to be asked jokingly never to do it again.

Tommy Bromilow, a strong half-back of the years after the First World War.

The manager of the Championship sides was David Ashworth, but he moved on to Oldham Athletic, who had finished bottom. Perhaps he realised the team were ageing. Matt McQueen, one of the 'Macs' from Liverpool's first teams of the nineties (but an Englishman), took over – he later completed the circle by becoming a director.

Liverpool slumped from these heights. They finished 12th next season, and although they remained in the First Division until the Second World War, they did not finish higher than fourth, and were usually round about the middle of the table. Their FA Cup record was appalling. In all those 20 seasons between the wars Liverpool could not get into even one semi-final. It began to be said that Liverpool would never win the Cup until the Liver bird fell off the Liver building. The local derbies with Everton began to be the highlights of the season, and old fans might well remember 7-4 and 6-0 victories over the old rivals in the 1930s.

The club was not short of famous players. In 1926 Gordon Hodgson came to England with a South African touring side. He remained to play for Liverpool, and three times for England. In ten seasons he scored 233 League goals, which was a Liverpool record until Roger Hunt passed it 30 years later. In the same season Liverpool signed Jimmy Jackson from Aberdeen, who later went into the church and was known as 'The Parson' to the terraces. Scots and South Africans became popular at Anfield – or rather Scots remained popular. Tom Bradshaw, centre-half in the Scottish 'Wembley Wizards' side of 1928 who beat England 5-1 at Wembley, joined Liverpool. Berry Nieuwenhuys came from South Africa to become a first-class winger. England's full-backs of many matches between 1928 and 1933, Tommy Cooper and Ernie Blenkinsop, were signed from Derby

Two Merseyside greats lead out their teams – Dixie Dean of Everton and Elisha Scott, the Liverpool goalkeeper.

International club football: Tom Bradshaw, the Liverpool skipper, handing a pennant to the FC Austria captain in 1934.

County and Sheffield Wednesday in 1935, and, although their international careers were over, tightened the defence. Ex-Irish international Sam English came from Rangers in 1933, and ex-English international Tom Johnson from Barrow in 1935 – both goal-scoring inside-forwards, but neither improved the goal famine among the forwards. The most famous ex-international signing was Matt Busby from Manchester City in 1935-36 – he played over 100 games for the Reds before war broke out.

Off the field, the Kop was rebuilt in 1928, and in 1935 George Kay, West Ham's captain in the first Wembley Cup Final of 1923, became Liverpool's first full-time manager, as opposed to secretary-manager.

Kay was still in charge when the full programme of League soccer began after the Second World War. Some of the players signed just before the war were available, notably Phil Taylor, Cyril Done, Jack Balmer, Bill Fagan, Bob Paisley and the greatest of them all, Billy Liddell. It could be argued that World Wars revive the fortunes of Liverpool, because in that first season they won their fifth Championship, and even reached the semi-final of the Cup before losing in a replay – it was a repeat of their only Cup Final, 1-0 to Burnley. The Championship was one of the closest ever, with Liverpool nine points behind Wolves with seven matches left – five of them away. The Reds dropped only one more point. When Liverpool played their last match, they were still behind Wolves and Stoke, and any of these teams could win the title. The Reds won 2-1 at Molyneux (a draw would have given Wolves the Championship) and then had to wait for Stoke. Stoke required to win their last match to take the title on goal average, but lost 2-1 at Sheffield United, so Liverpool won by a single point from Manchester United and Wolves, and by two points from Stoke City.

A new roof for the Anfield stadium in 1928.

The Liverpool squad was Sidlow, Lambert, Harley, Ramsden, Taylor, Jones W. H., Hughes, Paisley, Watkinson, Balmer, Stubbins, Done, Fagan, Liddell. Cyril Sidlow played seven times in goal for Wales and Ray Lambert five times at right-back; Jim Harley, a Scot, was a Powderhall Sprint Champion; Phil Taylor won a cap for England and later managed Liverpool; Laurie Hughes won three England caps; Bob Paisley later became the most successful Liverpool manager of all; Jackie Balmer, the captain, became in that season the first Football League player to score three hat-tricks in successive games; Albert Stubbins, signed for £12,500 (a big fee then) from Newcastle, was, for a couple of seasons, one of the hardest shots in the game and a popular symbol of Liverpool's new goal-scoring style, while Billy Liddell was a Merseyside legend whose career is outlined later in this book.

Stalwarts of the side which won the Championship in the first season after the Second World War. **Left** *Bob Paisley, later to be famous as a manager;* **top** *Albert Stubbins, a popular goal-scorer;* **above** *Bill Jones, solid in defence.*

*Previous pages The reception
for the losing 1950 Cup Finalists,
and, inset, King George VI
shaking hands with Liddell at
Wembley.*

Below *1950s manager Don
Welsh.*
Bottom *Louis Bimpson, a Welsh
signing.*

With such a strong squad, Liverpool had hopes of an extended run as contenders, but next season they dropped disappointingly to mid-table again, and they remained there for six seasons.

However, 1949-50 saw a Cup run at last, made all the sweeter by a defeat of Everton in the semi-final, 2-0 at Maine Road. Liverpool were in the final for the second time – the first being 36 years earlier – and were at Wembley for the first time. Arsenal were the opponents, which caused a problem, because their captain, Joe Mercer, who lived at Hoylake, had been training at Anfield. He was allowed to continue, but only at times when the Liverpool players weren't training.

Arsenal were an excellent side, with Logie their general, and on a rain-sodden pitch the teams played a classic game which Sir Stanley Rous said was one of the best finals he'd seen. Arsenal had the edge, however, and won 2-0 with two superb goals from Reg Lewis. It was Denis Compton's last big match. The Liverpool side was: Sidlow, Lambert, Spicer, Taylor (captain), Hughes, Jones, Payne, Baron, Stubbins, Fagan, Liddell. Some supporters thought Kevin Baron and Bill Jones were lucky to play. Baron and Bob Paisley had replaced the injured Jack Balmer and Bill Jones in previous games, Paisley actually scoring in the semi-final. With the injured players now fit, manager George Kay recalled Jones but Baron kept his place at Balmer's expense.

George Kay, a popular manager, retired after this match through ill-health. For a while Liverpool had been chasing the double, and the strain had begun to tell. Don Welsh, an England international who had enjoyed a long playing career with Charlton Athletic, took over, but Liverpool's League decline continued, with no more Cup runs for a while to alleviate the gloom.

In 1952-53 Liverpool avoided relegation only by beating Chelsea 2-0 in their last match, and they were knocked out of the FA Cup 1-0 by Gateshead. Alan A'Court, Louis Bimpson and Ronnie Moran all came to Liverpool, and all in their way served the club well later, but they could not halt the slide. The next season was a disaster, with Liverpool conceding 97 goals and finishing last. Bob Paisley and Phil Taylor retired to join the back room staff, and several new players were signed in a futile effort to stay up. Relegation was the more bitter since Everton, who had been relegated three seasons earlier, were promoted and took Liverpool's place.

Liverpool had been in the Second Division in three previous seasons, and each time had finished top of the table – but the last time was 50 years earlier, and Liverpool now found the Second Division an unfriendly place. One shock was what remains today their biggest-ever defeat, a 9-1 hammering by Birmingham City at St Andrews. Consolations were the form of veteran Billy Liddell, who scored 30 goals from centre-forward, and a fourth round Cup win at Everton by 4-0. But eleventh place in the Second Division still represents Liverpool's worst-ever season.

In 1955-56 there was some improvement, as Liverpool fought for promotion, just missing out in third place (in those days only two clubs were promoted). On top of this they lost to Manchester City in the FA Cup when Liddell's 'equalizer' went in after the referee had blown for time. Promotion was even closer the following season, when Liverpool were third again. Phil Taylor, their ex-captain and coach, had taken over as manager from Don Welsh, and he bought Tommy Younger, Scotland's goalkeeper from Hibernian, and Johnny Wheeler, a wing half from Bolton. Gerry Byrne made his debut as left-back, and with Geoff Twentyman and Ronnie Moran playing well at centre-half and right-back respectively, and a young Jimmy Melia on the books, things looked more promising. A 2-1

third-round defeat by Southend, however, emphasized Liverpool's poor Cup record.

Southend were third round opponents again in 1957-58 and Liverpool won this time 3-2, but only after a 1-1 draw at Anfield. Liverpool went on to the sixth round, eventually losing 2-1 at Blackburn. Although the Reds dropped to fourth in the League, they were only three points behind the winners, West Ham. Scoring was their problem. Although Liddell scored 22, the team managed only 79. Billy Liddell passed Elisha Scott's record of 429 League appearances, and another auspicious event came in October when the floodlights were switched on.

Liverpool were fourth again in 1958-59, but they were seven points off promotion, and never looked like going up. Billy Liddell was dropped for the first time, but even at 37 was too good to be left out permanently, and soon found himself back in the team. He wasn't playing when Liverpool suffered their worst Cup humiliation yet – they went out in the third round to Southern League side Worcester City. It was a time when even the keenest Liverpool supporters were close to despair. Had they but known it, the biggest defeat of the season held the clue to the great revival. Liverpool were thrashed 5-0 by Huddersfield Town. The Huddersfield manager was one Bill Shankly.

Tommy Younger, the Scottish international goalkeeper who joined the Reds in the mid-1950s.

The Shankly Years

Preceding pages *The idol of the Kop. Manager Bill Shankly acknowledges the adulation.*

Below *Shankly, left, supports his Preston captain after the 1938 FA Cup Final.*

'People say football's a matter of life and death for me. It isn't. It's much more important than that.'

This is one of the sayings of Bill Shankly, not as world-famous as the thoughts of Chairman Mao, perhaps, but legendary in football. Shankly-isms are like the Goldwynisms of the movie industry – they became so legendary that finally people were making them up for themselves. But it is true that Shankly was obsessed with football for seven days a week, and after 1 December 1959, football for Shankly meant Liverpool.

Bill Shankly was born in 1914 in Glenbuck, a Scottish mining village which has seen better days, but which even in its heyday never had more than about 1200 inhabitants. It was a breeding ground for footballers, however, and Shankly and his four older brothers all played for professional clubs. Bill played one season with Carlisle and then in 1933 was transferred to Preston North End.

A fit, non-stop right-half, Shankly played in the FA Cup Final of 1937 (Preston lost), and won a Cup-winner's medal in 1938, when Mutch scored a penalty in the last minute of extra time. In 1938 he won the first of five caps before the war interrupted his career. He won eight unofficial war-time caps and captained Scotland. He retired when Preston were relegated to the Second Division in 1949 and he lost his place to Tommy Docherty. Handing over the number 4 shirt after 16 years, he said to the Doc: 'You don't need to do anything with that – it runs around by itself'.

Super-fit Shankly was to say later he retired too early at 34. He went straight into management at Carlisle, and, in 1952, moved to Grimsby, then Workington, before becoming assistant at Huddersfield to Andy Beattie, who had been his captain at Preston. After a year Beattie became manager of Scotland, and Shankly was in charge of the once-famous Huddersfield Town. Huddersfield had come up from the Second Division in 1952-53, and next season, their first under Shankly, was their best for many years, finishing third in the Championship. Ironically, this was the season Liverpool were finally relegated to the Second Division.

Nobody mentions it now, but Huddersfield gradually sank down the table under Shankly, despite finding great players like Denis Law and Ray Wilson. They were relegated and even began to drop down the Second Division. Who knows what would have happened to Shankly had not his team inflicted that 5-0 defeat on Liverpool in 1958-59, his last season? Strange to relate, he had taken Huddersfield to the lowest-ever league position (14th in the Second Division) in their 49-year history.

Shankly had always claimed he would do well at a 'big' club (and was proved right), but his record with Huddersfield would not have suggested it. Even when the Liverpool directors went to sign him at a match between Cardiff and Huddersfield, Huddersfield lost. Shankly had applied for the Liverpool post some years before, at the time that Don Welsh was appointed, and had no hesitation in accepting the offer now.

Roger Hunt, Liverpool's most consistent scorer throughout the 1960s.

He began in revolutionary style. He decided that the back-room staff were of the calibre he required – Reuben Bennett was coach, Bob Paisley had just been promoted to first-team trainer and Joe Fagan was second team trainer. But some of the players had to go, and it is said that within a month or two Shankly had made a list of 24 dispensable men. Certainly 24 players had departed by the end of the following season.

In Shankly's first season, Roger Hunt and Ian Callaghan made their League debuts. Hunt scored 21 goals. Liverpool had a new goalkeeper, Bert Slater, and a new centre-forward, Dave Hickson, and Shankly signed Tommy Leishman from Hibernian to take over the central defensive role. Liverpool's performance was on a par with the previous season's – a distant third in the Second Division and an early Cup exit.

Next year the team-building continued, principally with the arrival of Gordon Milne, later to play for England. Billy Liddell played his final game, retiring with a Liverpool record of 492 League appearances. Gerry Byrne, who had been on the transfer list at Shankly's arrival, took over from Ronnie Moran at left-back, Moran switching to the right. The club's record was depressingly consistent, however, with another distant third place and another fourth-round Cup exit.

Jimmy Melia and Ronnie Moran, who were in the side which gained promotion from the Second Division in 1961-62.

Season 1961-62 was the breakthrough, and the beginning of Liverpool's extended run of success. It was based on what Shankly called his policy of building 'through the middle'. Jim Furnell came from Burnley to take over in goal, big Ron Yeats was bought from Dundee United for £30,000 to become a towering centre-half and Ian St John was signed for £35,000 from Motherwell to lead the attack.

The side were away to a brilliant start, scoring 21 points from the first 11 matches, with 31 goals against only four. Roger Hunt ended the season with 41 League goals, still a Liverpool record. The Second Division was won by eight points from Leyton Orient, and even in the Cup the fifth round was reached before Preston won on the second replay. There was a nasty incident at Derby, where Liverpool lost and the home team's Curry appeared to be roughed up both on and off the ball. This helped to give the Reds a reputation for a while of being tough and functional rather than artistic. But it was an excellent season. The team was Slater, then Furnell in goal, Moran and Byrne, Milne, Yeats and Leishman, Lewis, then Callaghan on one wing with A'Court on the other, and Hunt and Melia flanking St John in the centre.

Liverpool consolidated in their first season back in the top flight. Shankly developed his technique of giving his players a run-down on the opposition – the First Division stars which his players had not faced before. In Shankly's book each of them was faulty: 'He's past it; he's nursing an injury; he's over-rated; he's a homer' – and not to be compared with the Liverpool men, who strode on to the pitch as if they were giants. The Reds started badly, climbed to sixth and finally finished a satisfactory eighth. And, wonder of wonders, they reached the semi-final of the FA Cup, losing 1-0 to Leicester City.

The side was strengthened further this season. Willie Stevenson came from Rangers to take over from Leishman, but the most amazing coup was the promotion of Tommy Lawrence to the first team goal after five seasons in the reserves – he immediately won a Scottish cap and made the place his own for several seasons. The battles with Everton were resumed with two draws, with 70,000 at Anfield, and there were two amazing Easter games with Spurs, the 'double' team of two years earlier – a 5-2 victory and 7-2 defeat.

Willie Stevenson, a 1960s half-back capture from Rangers.

Tommy Lawrence, who after five years in Liverpool reserves, kept goal for Scotland.

The next season was the one for which the Liverpool faithful had been waiting for 17 years, although it began poorly. The side had been strengthened in the close season by the capture of winger Peter Thompson from Preston. Alf Arrowsmith emerged during the season as a goal-scorer, and St John took up a more constructive role, with Melia going to Wolverhampton. A strong run in the middle of the season took the Reds to the top of the table and the Championship was clinched with a couple of games to spare. Hunt, with 31 League goals, registered just over a third of Liverpool's 92 for the season. The Anfield faithful saw the new forward line four times score six at home, and twice five. The Cup provided its usual joke results, however. Liverpool just beat Third Division Port Vale 2-1, after a draw at Anfield, and in the sixth round lost 2-1 at Anfield to Swansea, who themselves escaped relegation to the Third Division by two points. Needless to say it was no joke to Shankly, whose gruff opinion was that the Reds should have won 14-0. The delighted Swansea manager corrected him: 14-2. This was one of the biggest shocks even for shock-prone Liverpool.

The Championship win meant Liverpool's first appearance in Europe – and Liverpool have played in European competitions in every season since. Perhaps, in the light of the severe competitiveness of the English League, this is their most remarkable feat of all.

Season 1964-65 was to be an interesting one in many ways. Liverpool began badly, with early season injuries and illnesses. They later fought their way up from near the foot of the table to seventh, but were never in contention to repeat their title win. There was nearly the most ridiculous result of all in the fourth round of the Cup. Liverpool, the Champions, were at home to Stockport County, destined to finish on the very bottom of the Fourth Division. Shankly went to Cologne to watch their European Cup opponents. In London on the way back he asked a porter if there had been any Cup shocks. Yes, he was told, Peterborough had beaten Arsenal. When Shankly saw the Liverpool result, 1-1, he nearly had apoplexy. But the Reds survived the replay, and, wonder of wonders, fought through to the Final. Their opponents were Leeds, who had just come up from the Second Division, and finished second in the Championship at their first attempt, and who were to be Liverpool's strongest rivals through to the 1970s.

Gordon Milne had been injured in the semi-final, and his place was taken by Geoff Strong, a utility player who had been signed from Arsenal. A rugged 19-year-old defender, Tommy Smith, had quickly won a place in the side, although usually wearing the number 10 shirt – the numbering associated with a 4-2-4 line-up was not easily being accepted in England. Chris Lawler, originally reserve centre-half to the immovable Yeats, had been given a run at right-back, and made the position his own, often scoring vital goals. The match at Wembley, a 2-1 win for the Reds after extra time, is described later in this book – suffice it to say that Ron Yeats collected the Cup, Shankly saluted the fans from the pitch, and the streets of Liverpool were packed for the victorious return on the open-topped bus. Liverpool had played the Cup Final in all-red strip, Shankly having earlier tried the red shorts instead of white in some earlier games. All-red was to be the Liverpool colours from then on.

Liverpool's march into Europe was not so happy, although it was not altogether their fault. They reached the semi-final on the toss of a coin (no penalty shoot-outs then) after three draws with Cologne. The semi-final was against mighty Inter Milan, the World Club Champions of the previous two years. The Reds won 3-1 at Anfield, with goals from Callaghan, Hunt and St John, but in the San Siro Stadium were robbed by two strange refereeing decisions – an Inter goal which went straight in from what appeared to be signalled as an indirect free kick, and another when Tommy Lawrence, preparing to take a goal kick, had the ball kicked from his hands. Inter Milan won the second leg 3-0. Liverpool also experienced a ploy which has been used again since. The night before the match the local church bells tolled (Shankly eventually stopped them), a band played, and car drivers blew their horns endlessly outside the players' hotel. It was all new to Liverpool, but it was experience gained, and never again were they to fall for the sucker punches of Continental opponents. Shankly was on the wrong end of a joke for a change when, on the way to Reykjavik for the European Cup first round, the team arrived at a holiday camp at Prestwick. 'We're going to Iceland' he said, and was told, 'I think you're on the wrong road.'

So the Reds had strung together two exceptional seasons and they continued the run in 1965-66. The team was now settled, and only 14 players were used throughout a League run which took them seven points clear of Leeds by the end of the season. Only 34 goals were conceded, 79 scored, with Hunt again at the top with 30. The Reds were to maintain this tight defence for the next few seasons, leading some frustrated opponents to call them boring. But no team could be boring with Thompson and Callaghan on the wings. The strongest team was Lawrence, Lawler, Byrne, Milne, Yeats, Stevenson, Callaghan, Hunt, St John, Smith, Thompson.

Chelsea knocked out the holders from the FA Cup 2-1 at Anfield in the third round, but Liverpool did better in their second season in Europe, reaching the final of the Cup Winners Cup. Some impressive names were listed among their victims: Juventus, Honved and Celtic, all despatched in second legs at Anfield after defeats or (in the case of Honved) a draw in the away legs. The final was against Borussia Dortmund at Glasgow, which should have favoured the Reds, with their Scots. But it was not the team's best night. Hunt scored, but it was 1-1 at 90 minutes, and a Ron Yeats own goal gave the Germans the Cup.

In the close season, Gerry Byrne, Roger Hunt and Ian Callaghan were in England's World Cup-winning squad for the finals – Peter Thompson and Gordon Milne were among the last to be discarded. Hunt played throughout, and Callaghan also got a game. Liverpool appeared in the Charity Shield for the third year running (they had held the shield jointly the previous seasons, with two draws) but this one was special, as their opponents, the FA Cup winners, were Everton and the Reds won 1-0 at Goodison.

The season itself, good enough for most teams, was a disappointment for Liverpool after three years of success. Gerry Byrne was injured early on, and never fully recovered. The side sank to fifth in the League, and Everton gained revenge for the Charity Shield defeat by removing the Reds 1-0 from the FA Cup. In the European Cup Liverpool came up against Ajax Amsterdam in the second round. Still four years from their consecutive triumphs, Ajax nevertheless were good enough to win 5-1 in Amsterdam and draw 2-2 at Anfield. The young Johan Cruyff was Liverpool's master.

Roger Hunt attacking the Borussia Dortmund goal in the 1966 European Cup Winners Cup Final in Glasgow. Despite a Hunt goal, Borussia won 2-1.

Following pages *Liverpool players celebrate the victory over Everton in the Charity Shield match of 1966. Ron Yeats, Roger Hunt, Peter Thompson and Ian St John lead the parade.*

Shankly bought 19-year-old Emlyn Hughes from Blackpool for Liverpool's then record fee of £65,000. Gordon Milne went the other way, and Willie Stevenson to Stoke, allowing Hughes to go into the team. In the close season Ray Clemence was signed from Scunthorpe, but with Lawrence playing so well he had to wait a couple of seasons before claiming his place. Tony Hateley, a tall centre-forward who was brilliant with his head, cost Liverpool £96,000 from Chelsea.

Two attackers of the late 1960s, Alun Evans, who cost Liverpool their first £100,000 fee, and **bottom,** *Bobby Graham.*

Liverpool finished third in the Championship in 1967-68, finishing only three points behind Manchester City, the winners. A long FA Cup run did not improve their prospects. Liverpool were forced to replays in each round between the third and sixth. Away draws were followed in each case by a win at Anfield, except in round six, when West Brom drew and then forced a win in the second replay. In this season the Reds were in the European Fairs Cup, and went out in the third round to Ferencvaros of Hungary, losing 1-0 home and away – many fans will still remember the brilliant volleyed goal which put them out at Anfield.

A £100,000 footballer joined Liverpool for the 1968-69 season – 18-year-old Alun Evans from Wolves. Shankly was giving the side a younger look. With two brilliant goalkeepers on the books, Lawrence and Clemence, the Liverpool defence conceded only 24 goals in the League – at the time a First Division record. No team scored more than two against them throughout the season, and only five managed even two. In each case, the two goals were enough to beat the Reds, however – Arsenal removing them from the Football League Cup and Bilbao from the European Fairs Cup, but only after the toss of a coin, each side winning 2-1 at home. Leicester City won 1-0 at Anfield in a fifth round FA Cup replay, so Liverpool performed only moderately in the Cups. The defence was unable to clinch the Championship, as Leeds became the dominant side in the country, and won by six clear points, the Reds being four points ahead of Everton in second place.

By now, Celtic and Manchester United had become the first British clubs to win the European Cup, so despite their successes of the 1960s, Liverpool were far from being supreme. More activity in the transfer market was required. Strangely, Shankly bought two defenders, Alec Lindsay from Bury and Larry Lloyd, a big centre-half in the Ron Yeats mould, from Bristol Rovers. Both went into the reserves. It became Liverpool policy to groom young players into the Anfield way of thinking before promoting them into the first team.

Liverpool had one of their most disappointing seasons for a few years in 1969-70. Roger Hunt finally came to the end of his top-flight career and went to Bolton Wanderers with Liverpool's League goal-scoring record of 245 goals. Ian St John was also near the end of his career. Alun Evans, after a bright start, had not established himself, and Tony Hateley had continued his football wanderings. Peter Thompson, Ian Callaghan and Bobby Graham did most of the attacking, but Liverpool scored only 65 goals. The defence conceded 42, with newly-promoted Derby County getting six without reply in their two games, and Manchester United scoring four at Anfield. Liverpool held on to fifth place to stay in Europe. Their European Fairs Cup campaign this season was disappointing, Setubal of Portugal winning on the away goals rule in the second round. Two away games with Second Division strugglers Watford resulted in a 2-1 League Cup win (but the Reds then went out in the third round) and a sixth-round 1-0 defeat in the FA Cup. Liverpool were still prone to Cup shocks.

Plainly something was required if Liverpool were to remain near the top in the 1970s. John Toshack was bought from Swansea for a club record £110,000 to spearhead the attack. Two young undergraduates, Steve

Heighway and Brian Hall, had already made their way to the forward line, and a local boy, John McLaughlin, played in mid-field. In the defence, Clemence took over permanently, while Lawler, Smith, Lloyd and Hughes were more or less ever-present. Lindsay eventually took over the left-back spot. Season 1970-71 was a transitional one for Liverpool, with Callaghan, Evans, Peter Thompson, Bobby Graham and Phil Boersma also playing their share of games. Of the old guard, Ian St John was dropped and went to coach in South Africa, Tommy Lawrence finally lost his place for good, while Yeats made a few appearances. It was the biggest change for some time. At the end of the season, Shankly paid £35,000 to Scunthorpe for Kevin Keegan, but he was to remain a reserve for some time yet.

The new-look side failed to find the consistency to improve upon the fifth place of the season before, but the settled defence once more restricted the opposition to only 24 goals, as two seasons earlier. Again no side scored more than two in any competition. The attack, however, was very poor, and only three times did the Reds themselves score more than two in the League. Only five First Division sides scored fewer than Liverpool's 42.

The Cup shock was got over in the League Cup, a 2-0 defeat by Swindon. But a semi-final defeat of Everton saw Liverpool at Wembley in the FA Cup Final. The opponents were Arsenal, and the match was a boring affair between two functional sides, strong in defence. There was no score at full-time, but two minutes into extra time Heighway scored with a shot inside the near post. But Arsenal withstood Wembley weariness better; Kelly equalized with a strange goal, and after the change of ends, George won it for Arsenal with a superb shot. It was Arsenal's 'double' year, but a major disappointment for Shankly. The team was: Clemence, Lawler, Lindsay, Smith, Lloyd, Hughes, Callaghan, Evans (Thompson), Heighway, Toshack, Hall. Liverpool got progressively better in the European Fairs Cup, finally despatching Bayern Munich before a semi-final goal by Leeds in the first leg at Anfield was enough to end the Reds' run.

Steve Heighway scores in extra time to give Liverpool the lead in the 1971 FA Cup Final, but Arsenal replied with two to take the Cup.

A new stand had been completed at Anfield in 1971, after many years in the planning and building. 'The ground is now fit for our great team and wonderful supporters,' said Shankly. The squad was more settled for the new season. The regular side was that which started the Cup Final, but with Keegan taking over from Evans. Ian Ross played 20 games in defence and local boy Phil Thompson made a late-season first appearance as a substitute. It was a disappointing season. Leeds, West Ham and Bayern Munich effected early disappearances from the FA, the League, and the European Cup Winners Cups respectively. A bad spell each side of Christmas spoiled a promising League challenge, but a string of seven wins left Liverpool approaching their last two games with an outstanding chance of the title. But they lost 0-1 at Brian Clough's Derby, which left Derby with 58 points. Leeds had 57 and Liverpool 56, each with a game to play and a better goal average than Derby. Leeds needed a draw to take the Championship, Liverpool could do it with a win. Leeds lost at Wolves (thereby throwing away the double), but Liverpool could only draw 0-0 at Highbury, to finish third. Derby won the title while on holiday in Majorca.

Season 1972-73 was Liverpool's best yet. Scottish international Peter Cormack was signed from Nottingham Forest, and claimed a place in the side, mainly at the expense of Hall or Toshack, while Boersma played 19 games up front and Phil Thompson twelve in defence. Keegan and Toshack established their goal-scoring partnership, finishing with 13 each in the League, with Keegan's 22 being top overall. Liverpool went to the top of the table on 24 September with a 5-0 win over Sheffield United and stayed top to the end, finishing three points clear of Arsenal. Manchester City and Spurs put the Reds out of the FA Cup and League Cup but the side had a 100

Typical action from Kevin Keegan in the early 1970s, scoring with a diving header.

per cent record in the home legs of the UEFA Cup, as the old Fairs Cup was now called. After a semi-final against Spurs won only on the principle of the goal scored by Heighway at White Hart Lane counting double, Liverpool found themselves against Borussia Moenchengladbach in the final. The Anfield leg was abandoned after half an hour because a downpour made the pitch unfit – a good decision for Liverpool, as Keegan (2) and Lloyd opened up a 3-0 lead in the replay. Liverpool took the Cup, won the previous year by Spurs, to Germany for the second leg, and nearly left it there as a Gunter Netzer-inspired Borussia led 2-0 at half-time. But the defence held out, and it was realized that a penalty save by Clemence in the first leg had been vital. Liverpool's winning side was: Clemence, Lawler, Lindsay, Smith, Lloyd, Hughes, Keegan, Cormack, Heighway, Toshack, Callaghan, with Hall and Boersma being substituted for Heighway, one in each leg.

So Liverpool tasted European success for the first time, and in 1973-74 were in the European Cup, which was by now the target Liverpool had set their sights on. The Reds slipped up, however, and at Anfield of all places. A 2-1 defeat by Red Star Belgrade in the second round first leg did not seem too serious, but Red Star came to Anfield and attacked, and won again by 2-1. It was hard luck on Chris Lawler, who scored both goals. Phil

A top deck full of cups for a top-class team. Liverpool parading their trophies in 1972-73, when they had their first European success – the UEFA Cup.

Thompson had come into the side in place of Tommy Smith, who was considered near retirement, but Smith continued to play so well he found himself a new niche, taking over at right-back from the luckless Lawler. Lloyd missed the second half of the season, and Toshack, Hall and Boersma continued to fight for one or two places in attack or midfield.

The League programme was disappointing, too. Liverpool won their way to second place by December, but thereafter could make no impression on Leeds, who led the table throughout the season. The FA Cup saved the season, but the giant-killing jinx nearly worked again. Perhaps there was something wrong with the Kop that season. Doncaster Rovers, who finished one point off the bottom of the Fourth Division, were only eliminated after a 2-2 draw at Anfield, and Second Division Carlisle also drew at Anfield before losing the replay. The Reds also needed two attempts to dispose of struggling Leicester City in the semi-final, but in the final they were superb. In a match described later, the Reds annihilated Newcastle 3-0.

Bill Shankly bought Ray Kennedy from Arsenal for £200,000 and then shocked the football world on 12 July 1974 by announcing his retirement. Perhaps the European Cup disappointment influenced him. Perhaps he decided to go on a high after the brilliant Cup Final display. There were stories of disagreements with the board, and certainly after a time he became a rare visitor to the club. He had lived for Liverpool and football. One of the best-known stories about him concerns a rare day off to take out his wife Nessie for a wedding anniversary treat – to watch Rochdale reserves. It is certainly untrue, and he disposed of the story with his usual joke: 'Would I have got married in the football season?'

Shankly's devotion had revitalized Liverpool. From a struggling club he had made them into one of the most successful in the land. He had given the players pride and inspired the spirit that refused to give in. He would not tolerate a lack of effort or of discipline, either on or off the field. Under him Liverpool became famous as a side likely to win matches in the last five minutes, when other sides might be looking forward to the shower bath and a beer. The fans loved him as a Messiah, and when they kissed his feet on the Wembley turf he did not regard it as over-enthusiasm.

Shankly shocked the football world again on 28 September 1981 when he died after just a few days in hospital. He had seemed indestructible. He is remembered now in the Shankly Gates at Anfield, but it will be years before the fans need such a memorial to remind them of his reign as manager.

Opposite *The fans pay homage to Bill Shankly, the man who pointed Liverpool towards the heights.*

'You'll never walk alone' *is the message on Anfield's Shankly Gates.*

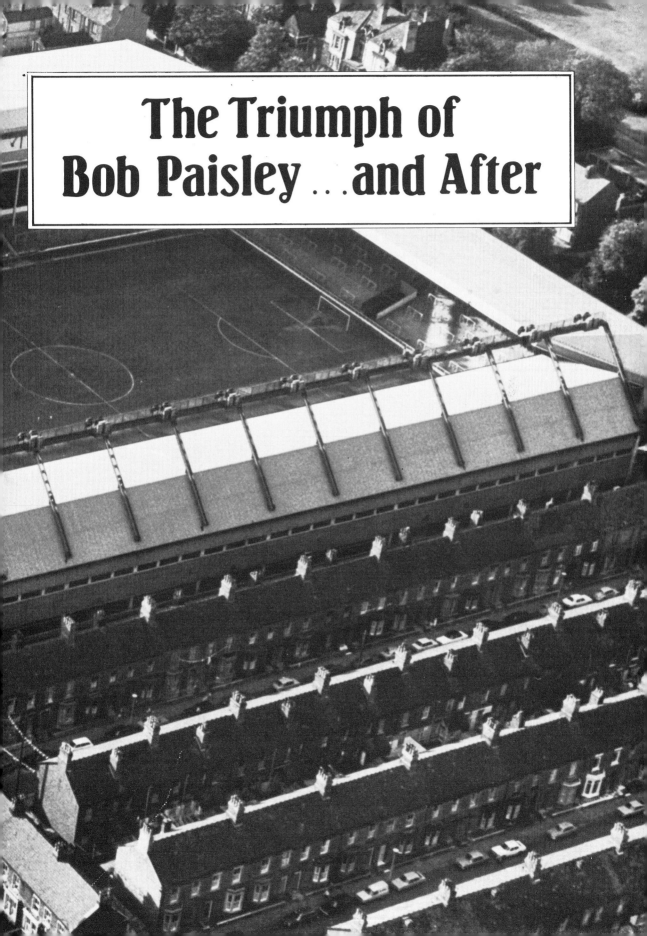

The Triumph of
Bob Paisley ...and After

Preceding pages *The modern Anfield stadium from the air.*

Bob Paisley receiving the Football League Milk Cup in 1983, the last of his successes as manager.

When Shankly retired there was a long-serving back-room team at Liverpool, whose loyalty to the club was no less committed than Shankly's. Rather than bring in a new charismatic figure, the club decided to move everybody up a peg. It was thought to be Shankly's idea.

Bob Paisley, Shankly's right-hand man, became the new manager. Joe Fagan, from the coaching staff, was to become the assistant manager, and Ronnie Moran the first-team trainer.

Paisley was the opposite of charismatic. He had joined Liverpool in 1939, and fought in the war. He won a League Championship medal when football resumed in 1946-47 and Liverpool finished top. His big disappointment as a player came in 1950, when he was left out of the Cup Final team. At this time he felt he was in the running for an England cap.

Unlike Shankly, Paisley was a man of few words. He enjoyed a quiet life with his family, and had a strong interest outside football in horses, being a friend of race-horse trainers Frankie Durr and Frankie Carr. Not being a natural talker, he was initially ill at ease before the television cameras and mistrusted the press. In his autobiography he suspected that the press dubbed him 'shrewd old Uncle Bob' to cover up his shortcomings. It was nevertheless an accurate description. He might not have been a source of firecracker quotes like Shankly, nor was he one for the flamboyant gesture from the bench, being usually seen watching matches impassively from the privacy of the box. But so far as the football was concerned, shrewd he was, having witnessed and learnt from the ups and downs and comings and goings at Anfield for 35 years.

Not all observers thought his appointment was wise. There were those who thought Shankly could never be adequately replaced. Others thought that Paisley was chosen to keep the ship on an even keel until another big name could take over. He was, after all, 54 years old. Most expected a decline in Liverpool's fortunes, for a while at least.

At first they were right, or at least half-right. The team were always in the first six in the table, and led near the end, but finished second to Derby by two points. They did nothing in the Cups, going out in the second round of the European Cup Winners Cup, after two draws with old rivals Ferencvaros, whose away goal at Anfield settled it. Phil Neal, bought from Northampton, took over in mid-season at left back from Lindsay, Kennedy shared the number 10 shirt with Toshack, and Terry McDermott, bought from Newcastle after the Cup Final, played 14 games. Jimmy Case, a local player, made his debut in the last match of the season.

Apart from the Charity Shield, won on penalties after an ill-tempered draw with Leeds, in which Keegan and Bremner were sent off, threw down their shirts in disgust and were suspended for 11 matches, Liverpool did not win a trophy. If this was thought to be the beginning of a slide, Paisley's second season proved the doubters wrong. The Reds led the table, faltered, and came with a late run of eight wins and a draw from the last nine matches to pip Queen's Park Rangers by one point. And although the FA Cup and League Cup saw quick exits, the double of three years earlier was repeated when Liverpool added the UEFA Cup to the Championship. After struggling to beat Hibs, they squeezed past Dynamo Dresden (another penalty save by Clemence made the difference) and then scored a famous victory before 80,000 in Barcelona, Cruyff and Neeskens included. Toshack's goal meant that a 1-1 draw at Anfield was good enough to reach the final against Bruges. All looked lost when at Anfield Bruges took a 2-0 half-time lead, but Kennedy, Case and a Keegan penalty gave the Reds a narrow lead to take to Belgium. When Bruges levelled the aggregate after 11 minutes, it seemed their away goals might decide it, but Keegan equalized to give Liverpool the Cup.

Clemence and Neal were ever-present in the side; Joey Jones, bought from Wrexham, and Alex Lindsay contested the other full-back spot until Tommy Smith made it his half-way through the season. Phil Thompson and Hughes were almost ever-present, while Kennedy took over the number 5 shirt from Cormack in mid-season, and played in a similar manner as an advancing mid-fielder. Keegan, Heighway, Toshack and Callaghan were regular attackers, while McDermott started at inside-forward, but lost his place to Hall, who in turn lost it to Case. Meanwhile, in the final triumphant run at the end of the season, David Fairclough, a red-headed local player, made his first appearances and played over ten times as substitute, scoring vital goals and earning himself the title (which he found it impossible to lose) of 'super-sub'.

The team began 1976-77 in the manner they ended the previous one. This was Liverpool's finest season. The squad was now settled. Apart from three appearances by two other players, only 15 men were called upon for the League programme. One was the only new arrival, David Johnson, an England centre-forward who came via Everton and Ipswich. By September the team led the division, and although headed once or twice thereafter by Ipswich, won the title when Ipswich folded up at the end of the season. Even with three draws and a defeat in their last four games the Reds held on to win by a point from Manchester City.

After clinching the title, Liverpool were due to play Manchester United in the FA Cup Final, and four days later Borussia Moenchengladbach in the European Cup Final in Rome. A unique treble was on the cards. Alas for Liverpool, the second part of the treble went wrong. Paisley was bitter

Terry McDermott was one of the Liverpool regulars from the mid-1970s.

David Fairclough, the 'super-sub' who scored many vital goals.

before and after the match about an FA decision to replay the Cup Final, if drawn, on June 27 – during Wimbledon fortnight. The imminence of the European Final required some scheduling decision, of course, but to a team chasing a treble, the prospect of remaining in training almost until the next season started was, he thought, a damaging psychological blow. Be that as it may, Liverpool were firm favourites. They were also the better side. After 50 minutes Stuart Pearson surprised Clemence with a shot under the goalkeeper's body at the near post. All seemed to be on course, however, when two minutes later Case scored a splendid goal from the edge of the box. But after another three minutes, United scored a fortunate goal. A mistake by Smith allowed Jimmy Greenhoff a shot, the ball rebounded off a defender, Macari swung his foot, the ball hit Greenhoff and lobbed gently into the net with Clemence deceived and Neal, rushing back, unable to get there. Thereafter Liverpool pressed, United defended, but no more goals would come. At the end of the match, Paisley was on the pitch lifting the spirits of his dejected men. The biggest match of all was yet to come.

How Liverpool went to Rome and triumphed in the best European Cup Final from that day to this is described later. Seven players played in nearly all matches that season: Clemence, Neal, Jones, Kennedy, Hughes, Keegan and Heighway. Thompson was injured after 26 matches, and Smith took over. Callaghan and Toshack lost their places towards the end of the season, but Callaghan came back in Rome. Johnson, Case, Fairclough and McDermott were the four others who made up the successful fifteen.

Jimmy Case scores a spectacular equalizer in the 1977 FA Cup Final against Manchester United.

46

There was a crucial departure from Anfield before the next season. Kevin Keegan, having made it known that he had ambitions to play in Europe, was transferred to Hamburg for £500,000. It might have been a bitter blow, but Paisley realised that the best way to overcome such a loss was to buy a top-class player as a straight replacement. Scottish international Kenny Dalglish was signed from Celtic for £440,000. Keegan had cost Shankly only £35,000. Both buys were equally inspired. They became the driving force of Liverpool, one following the other and between them keeping the Reds at the fore of English soccer for a dozen years.

Despite his compact squad and their success, Paisley realized that some of the other established players were getting old, and he had learned that building is best done when the team is at the top. Three other important newcomers, apart from Dalglish, made their appearances in 1977-78. Alan Hansen came from Partick Thistle and established himself, first in midfield, then in defence. Then Scottish international Graeme Souness was bought from Middlesbrough and, wearing the number 10 or 11 shirt, began to play strongly in mid-field. The Scottish influence was getting stronger, but local talent was represented by young Sammy Lee, who made his first two League appearances as a substitute. David Johnson and John Toshack, on the other hand, made only a handful of appearances. Strangely the older players kept going – Callaghan played 25 League games before Souness took over, and Smith, deputizing at first for Thompson, later took over at back from Joey Jones. McDermott gained a regular place, and Fairclough came

off the bench and played 26 matches as first choice. Dalglish and Neal were the only league ever-present, but Clemence, Kennedy and Hughes missed only six matches between them, and Case and Heighway played in most of the games.

In the Championship, Liverpool moved up and down in the top six, fitting all positions except first. Having finally shaken off Leeds as their most consistent challengers, the Reds found new and awkward pretenders to English soccer supremacy in newly promoted Nottingham Forest. Forest quickly went to the top, and to everybody's surprise kept going, not losing a League match after November. Liverpool finished seven points behind in second place.

An inspired Chelsea removed the Reds from the FA Cup in the third round, but Liverpool fought through to the final of the League Cup, which provided a showdown with upstarts Forest. There was a goalless draw at Wembley and Forest's well-organized defence shut-out the Liverpool forwards again in the replay at Old Trafford. Forest scored a controversial winner from the penalty spot when Thompson brought down O'Hare, who was through and bearing down on Clemence. The TV replay showed the trip was just *outside* the area. Commentator Brian Moore made the most of it, and Thompson, in the disappointment of the moment, was led into injudicious remarks about the decision, and charged with bringing the game into disrepute. Paisley thought Liverpool were hard done by in both matches, but the dispute was bad publicity for Liverpool, and an acceptance that for the moment Forest had an Indian sign on them would have served them better.

However, the season was not lost. The best way to top the winning of the European Cup was to win it again, and the Reds did just that. Their old rivals Borussia Moenchengladbach were potential stumbling blocks in the semi-final, especially when a last minute goal gave them a 2-1 home win in the first leg. But the Reds were superb at Anfield, and goals by Kennedy, Dalglish and Case earned a Wembley final with Bruges. A superb Dalglish goal won a second successive European Cup for Liverpool.

A hat-trick of European Cups was not to be, however. A cruel draw matched the European Champions with the League Champions in the first round the following season, and again Liverpool found that Forest had the edge. A policy of containment at Nottingham went wrong when Forest scored late to take a 2-0 lead to Anfield. For the fourth time in important Cup games Liverpool could not score against them and a 0-0 draw took Forest through. They went on to take the European Cup themselves.

An early exit in the League Cup left Liverpool just the traditional double to go for, and that nearly disappeared immediately when in the third round of the FA Cup, the Reds could only draw 0-0 at Third Division Southend. However, the semi-final was reached and provided two terrific games with Manchester United. At Maine Road, McDermott missed a penalty and it took a late goal by Hansen to earn Liverpool a 2-2 draw and a replay at Goodison Park, where they were clear favourites. Perhaps they were over-confident. They had an off-day and United won 1-0.

Liverpool were supreme in the Championship, though. Starting with ten wins and a draw in the first 11 matches, they just strode away from the rest and were never challenged. On 16 April Aston Villa beat them 3-1, the only team to score more than one against them in the League all season. The 'indignity' was corrected on 8 May, when Liverpool beat Villa 3-0 at Anfield to make sure of the title. They conceded only 16 goals, a record for any division of the League. Liverpool finished eight points clear of Forest.

In this season, Liverpool used only 13 men, apart from four appearances by Fairclough or Lee. They were: Clemence, Neal, Alan Kennedy, who had been signed from Newcastle to take over the left-back spot, Thompson, Ray Kennedy, Hughes, Dalglish, Case, Heighway, McDermott, Souness, Johnson and Hansen. Toshack had left to manage Swansea, and Callaghan and Smith went to play for him in the Second Division. Emlyn Hughes, captain in both European Cup wins, made the last of his 474 League appearances and was transferred to Wolves. A curiosity was the arrival of Frank McGarvey from St Mirren, who earned two Scottish caps and departed for Celtic without making a League appearance for Liverpool.

Season 1979-80 was strangely typical for Liverpool. There was a successful League campaign, dour Cup struggles with Nottingham Forest, and a long drawn out FA Cup semi-final. The results were typical, too. The Forest encounter came in the semi-final of the League Cup. In the first leg at Nottingham, Forest took a 1-0 lead. At Anfield Liverpool, through Fairclough, finally scored against Forest, but Forest scored too, and went to the final on aggregate. Between the two legs Liverpool went to Nottingham again in the FA Cup and won 2-0. Eventually they found themselves playing Arsenal in the semi-final. On 12 April the teams drew 0-0 at Hillsborough, on 16 April 1-1 at Villa Park, after extra time, on 28 April 1-1 at Villa Park again, after extra time, and on 1 May Arsenal finally beat Liverpool 1-0.

The side began poorly in the League, winning only two of their first seven games, but by 8 December they reached the top to stay, finishing two points clear of Manchester United. The European Cup was a shock for the Reds, however. Dynamo Tbilisi, the Russian champions, played superbly at Anfield, and were unlucky to lose 2-1, but before 80,000 of their own supporters they outplayed Liverpool in the return leg 3-0, and the Reds exited in the first round. The side which played practically throughout the League season was Clemence, Neal, Kennedy A, Thompson, Kennedy R, Hansen, Dalglish, Case, Johnson, McDermott, Souness. Avi Cohen, an Israel international full-back, had joined the club and made three League appearances, while new names on the books were Ron Whelan, local boy Colin Irwin and Ian Rush, a Welsh international bought from Chester.

The Reds were slightly less impressive in the first season of the 1980s. Too many home points were dropped in the League, and 12 away games were drawn. Fifth was their worst position for ten years, and they hadn't finished lower for 16 years. After a third round FA Cup win over non-League Altrincham, where old favourite Brian Hall was in the opposing team, there was a disappointing fourth round defeat by Everton. But the unimpressive Reds took two trophies.

In the League Cup, they lost 1-0 to a side in the bottom half of the Fourth Division, Bradford City, in the second round, but luckily this round was still over two legs, and the Reds went through to the final. The opponents were West Ham, who got a late penalty to equalize 1-1 at Wembley, but in the replay at Villa Park Liverpool got progressively better as the match went on, and after they'd gone ahead 2-1, West Ham could not come back. So one Cup was in the bag, and meanwhile the European Cup was coming to a climax.

Liverpool steamed through to the semi-final with convincing wins in both legs against Aberdeen and CSKA Sofia (who removed twice-champions Nottm Forest), as well as a 10-1 win at Anfield against Finnish amateurs OPS Oulu. In the semi-final the Reds were held at Anfield 0-0 by Bayern Munich, and the German side thought this would be enough. Paul Breitner unwisely stated this opinion openly and further remarked that Liverpool were an unimaginative side. If this was meant to dispirit the

Reds, it had the opposite effect. They gave one of their best performances in the second leg, with reserves Richard Money and Colin Irwin in the side. Dalglish, not fully fit, was injured almost immediately, and Howard Gayle, a local player, came on to run at Bayern – when he was exhausted Case came on for him. It was old hand Ray Kennedy who settled the match, taking a centre from David Johnson a few minutes from the end and with calm deliberation placing the ball home. That Karl-Heinz Rummenigge equalized in the last minute was academic – the away goal was enough.

The team painted Paris 'Red' on 27 May when they won the final (described later) 1-0, to become the fourth side to register three wins. In this successful season Sammy Lee made himself a regular in mid-field, while Fairclough, Money, Irwin, Cohen and Rush also played in a few games. Jimmy Case played 14 League games and was ten times on as a substitute. New players on the books included goalkeeper Bruce Grobbelaar from Rhodesia, via the unlikely route of Crewe Alexandra and Vancouver Whitecaps, and Craig Johnston from Johannesburg, via the equally unlikely Lake McQuarrie, Sydney City and Middlesbrough. Steve Heighway was allowed to go in April, having made regular first team appearances right up to the last month.

In the close season Ray Clemence, still at the top of his form, was transferred to Spurs to make way for the younger Grobbelaar. With the departure of Heighway and Clemence the last playing links with the Shankly sides had departed.

The European Cup in 1981-82 was disappointing. The unfortunate Finns of OPS Oulu were again despatched comprehensively, and AZ 67 of Holland narrowly, but CSKA Sofia held Liverpool to a 1-0 result at Anfield, and in the second leg won 2-0 after extra time. Aston Villa went on to keep the Cup

in England for the sixth successive year. In the FA Cup, the Reds found that Chelsea, now in the Second Division, were still a hoodoo team, and lost in the fifth round 2-0 at Stamford Bridge.

Yet again, two trophies came to Anfield, however. Just before the European Cup disappointment, the Reds had faced Tottenham Hotspur in the League Cup Final. In an excellent match, described later, the Reds beat Spurs 3-1, putting the last two past Ray Clemence in extra time. By then the Championship was well won, Liverpool following a home defeat by Brighton on 6 March with 11 successive wins, continuing unbeaten to the end of the season, and winning by four points from Ipswich. This was the first season of three points for a win, so their total of 87 points was naturally a record. Remarkably, once more only 15 players had been used, plus two appearances by a substitute. Jimmy Case had gone to Brighton and Colin Irwin to Swansea. Ray Kennedy left in January to join the growing Liverpool clan at Swansea. David Johnson and McDermott lost their places during the season, and Johnston, Whelan and Rush came into the side. Mark Lawrenson, a defender signed from Brighton, claimed a regular place from the start. The other eight, more or less regulars, were Grobbelaar, Neal, Thompson, Hansen, Dalglish, Lee, Souness and Alan Kennedy. Avi Cohen and super-sub Fairclough left during the season.

Liverpool's season in 1982-83 can be summed up quickly. It was identical to the previous season. The same round was reached in the FA Cup, the fifth, but it was one of the shocks of the season when the Reds lost, reminiscent of the old days. Brighton, who were to finish bottom of the division, came to Anfield and won 2-1. The game was played on Sunday, and Brighton led 1-0 at half-time. Johnston equalized, but old Liverpool favourite Jimmy Case hit a late winner, with Neal missing a penalty chance

Ian Rush gained a place in the 1981-82 season, and was soon slotting in goals.

to equalize. Brighton's manager was another old Liverpool player, Jimmy Melia.

The European Cup was also lost in the same round – the quarter-final. Widzew Lodz won the first leg in Poland 2-0, and even here a Grobbelaar mistake duplicated the previous season's mishap. At Anfield, Liverpool led, but Souness gave away a penalty, Liverpool pressed but Lodz broke away to score again, and Liverpool, now needing four more, could manage only two, one probably off-side.

So Liverpool were left with their usual two trophies. There were no problems on the way to the Milk Cup Final, against Manchester United. Whiteside gave United an early lead, but Liverpool pressure wore down the opposition and Alan Kennedy equalized with a long shot to force extra time. United had several injured players thereafter and it was only a matter of time before Whelan struck the winner with a long swerving shot.

Liverpool had the Championship sewn up from a long way out, to win their seventh title in 11 seasons. It was won so early that the Reds eased down and suffered five defeats and two draws in their last seven matches, but still finished 11 points clear of Watford. The only newcomer to earn a regular place in the side was Dave Hodgson, bought from Middlesbrough for £450,000. But super-sub Fairclough returned and made three League appearances plus five as a substitute.

When the Milk Cup was won, manager Paisley was pushed into accepting it. It was a sentimental gesture, because Bob Paisley had announced his retirement from the end of the season. There was no real reason – he had just done enough. And when you add it all up, it is certainly enough. In nine seasons, he won six Championships, three League Cups, one UEFA Cup and, perhaps best of all, three European Cups. Thirteen trophies in nine seasons. It is a pity he did not win an FA Cup, especially after missing the final in 1950, a disappointment which he still feels.

Bob Paisley, OBE, joined the Liverpool board, an honour denied Shankly. His assistant, Joe Fagan, took over as manager for 1983-84.

He made a poor start, when Liverpool lost the Charity Shield to Manchester United, but Paisley was reckoned to have made a poor start when Liverpool finished second in the table in his first season. Fagan inherited a youngish popular side, and it wasn't long before the Reds (by now often called the Super-Reds) had climbed to the top of the table again.

As the season progressed, Manchester United emerged as the only serious challengers in the Championship. For two weeks in March United actually topped the table, but Liverpool drew ahead again on 31 March and thereafter, whenever they dropped a point or two, United did likewise. The Reds were eventually easy winners by three points from Southampton.

By winning the Championship for the third successive year, Liverpool equalled the feats of Huddersfield Town and Arsenal, the only other clubs to achieve this, in the 1920s and 1930s respectively. But Liverpool's performance in being champions in seven of nine consecutive seasons is by far the most outstanding by any club since the Football League started.

Steve Nicol, a Scottish Under-21 player who had joined the club from Ayr United for £300,000, began to make useful appearances in the first team, and Michael Robinson, a burly centre forward, was signed from Brighton, and often appeared as a substitute. When Liverpool began to look fallible in March 1984, John Wark was signed from Ipswich, and scored in his first game – a win which took Liverpool back to the top of the table for the rest of the season.

At the end of March, Liverpool won their fourth consecutive Milk Cup – the first time any club had won a major trophy four times in succession. The

Joe Fagan's happy smile as he took over the top job at Anfield in 1983. He resigned two years later at the end of an unhappy 1984-85 season.

victory in a replayed final with Everton is described later.

Manager Joe Fagan's first season was therefore one of triumph – Liverpool chalked up another milestone by becoming the first club to win three major trophies in one season.

Season 1984-85 was marked by disaster – not disaster only in football language, but real tragedy. As this is a book about football, the ordinary events of the season must be dealt with first.

Before the season started, the captain, Graeme Souness, left the club to join Sampdoria in Italy. Phil Neal became the new club captain. Two players made their debut at the start of the league season, Paul Walsh, an England striker bought from Luton Town for £750,000, and Jan Molby, a Danish international midfielder bought from Ajax Amsterdam for £225,000. Neither player established a regular place throughout the season. Jim Beglin, an Irish full back from Shamrock Rovers, Gary Gillespie, a £325,000 defender from Coventry, and Kevin MacDonald, a Scot from Inverness who was transferred from Leicester City, made their debuts later in the season.

Kevin MacDonald, previously with Leicester City, joined Liverpool during the 1984-85 season.

Results on the field did not at first improve much from the opening Charity Shield fixture, a 1-0 defeat by Everton. On 20 October, when Everton repeated that score-line at Anfield in the League, the Reds were sixth from the bottom of the table, and at one point they were next to bottom. That they recovered from there to finish second says much for their character. Before or during the season David Hodgson, Michael Robinson and former captain Phil Thompson left the club.

In the domestic Cups, Liverpool lost their four-year hold on the Milk Cup when losing 1-0 at Tottenham in the third round. In the FA Cup, the semi-final was reached, but an equalizer four minutes from the end and another equalizer in the last minute of extra time against Manchester United to make the score 2-2 only brought a replay, in which two second-half United goals turned a half-time Liverpool lead into a 2-1 defeat.

Everybody was hoping that the season would be saved by the European Cup, in which Liverpool played some of their best football of the season. Lech Poznan were beaten 5-0 on aggregate, Benfica 3-2, Austria Vienna 5-2 and Panathinaikos 5-0 to set up a final against Juventus at the Heysel Stadium in Brussels.

Shortly before the match was due to start, a body of Liverpool 'supporters' charged into an enclosure containing mostly Juventus fans, driving the fleeing Italians into a corner where a wall collapsed, causing panic and confusion which led to 38 deaths and hundreds of injuries.

After a delay of over an hour, the match went ahead (to prevent further rioting) and Liverpool lost 1-0. It was a good match in the circumstances and Liverpool were possibly the better side, but two penalty decisions decided the result – Juventus were awarded one when Boniek was tripped outside the area and Liverpool refused one when Whelan was tripped inside (although it must be said Boniek was robbed of the better chance of scoring).

The disaster at last provoked UEFA to move against persistent English soccer hooliganism. All English sides were banned from the European competitions indefinitely (after the FA had pusillanimously withdrawn for a season). Later FIFA went further, and banned all English clubs from playing abroad at all.

Before the final, Joe Fagan had announced his resignation as manager, stating he was tired and too old. After the tragedy he said he looked forward in sorrow and disgust to his departure from the game.

Kenny Dalglish was announced as the new manager, while still holding a contract as a player. It was said that the previous manager, Bob Paisley, who was now a director, would advise Dalglish in the early stages.

So the glorious years of Liverpool's involvement in European football came to an end not through deficiencies on the pitch (the Reds had qualified for the 1985-86 UEFA Cup) but through deficiencies in a section of their 'fans'. The club which brought pride to city and country had now brought shame, disgrace and humiliation. The players and the real fans were sickened. Grobbelaar was only one player who considered giving the game up altogether.

Dalglish and the team therefore began the 1985-86 season with a huge task before them. Without a major trophy for the first time in ten years, and with European competition barred, the only way Liverpool could regain their supremacy was to win the Championship, and, if possible, one of the domestic cups as well. Anything less and the talk would be of the 'end of an era' kind. Dalglish included himself in the team in the first match and played well as Arsenal were overcome 2-0 before 38,261 spectators at Anfield. A pre-match service reminded all present of the tragedy of the previous year. In the second match (in which Rush missed a penalty in a 2-2 draw at Villa Park), Dalglish omitted himself, giving Paul Walsh the chance to build a partnership with Rush. The side at the beginning of the season was: Grobbelaar, Neal, Kennedy, Lawrenson, Whelan, Hansen, Walsh, Nicol, Rush, Molby, Beglin.

The first defeat arrived in the third match, 1-0 at Newcastle, where Dalglish played. Craig Johnston and Sammy Lee appeared in a 5-0 thrashing of Ipswich. As the season progressed, and Liverpool settled down in the top half of a League table being dominated by Manchester United, who won their first ten games, Dalglish preferred to play himself only in important games. Steve McMahon, a Liverpool-born midfield player, who had preferred Aston Villa to Liverpool when transferred from Everton in 1983, had now been brought to Anfield and came into the first team.

In a match for the Screen Sport Super Cup (a very forgettable competition introduced for English teams which would have played in Europe) Dalglish dropped the veteran full-backs, Neal and Kennedy, for the new younger partnership of Nicol and Beglin. They played well, and were retained for the League visit to Goodison, where Liverpool beat the Champions 3-2, Dalglish, Rush and McMahon scoring. Liverpool moved into second spot in the table, nine points behind United.

Phil Neal regained his full-back place and John Wark came into the side for a Milk Cup match at Oldham, most notable for the fact that both Oldham goals were scored by David Fairclough, the Reds' former 'super-sub'.

Nicol returned at full-back for the Championship visit to Old Trafford. With Dalglish injured in training, the team was: Grobbelaar, Nicol, Beglin, Lawrenson, Whelan, Hansen, Wark, Molby, Rush, Johnston, McMahon. Molby played deep, with the full-backs encouraged to attack.

In the manager's absence, this appeared to be the preferred side after a quarter of the season. Wark, who was to have a bad season with injuries, collected another and Walsh returned in his place. Kevin MacDonald was the regular substitute. Liverpool drew this match 1-1, and in November put United out of the Milk Cup. By then United's season had begun to fall apart, and Liverpool had closed the gap in the title race to two points.

Liverpool themselves began to slip, however. A draw at Nottingham Forest is interesting in retrospect because the side fielded was the eventual Cup Final team. Everton and Chelsea passed them, and when United were at last toppled from their perch, it was Everton who went to the top.

Gary Gillespie began to figure regularly in the team from January. The

Milk Cup and FA Cup campaigns proceeded satisfactorily, the latter with a televised Sunday afternoon victory at Stamford Bridge.

On 22 February, a 2-0 defeat by Everton at Anfield looked to have ended the Reds' title prospects – they were now eight points behind their local rivals with 12 games to play. They had struggled to beat Third Division York City after extra time in an FA Cup replay, and soon they went out of the Milk Cup semi-final to Queen's Park Rangers. A 1-0 defeat at Loftus Road seemed to make the Anfield leg almost a formality, but silly own-goals from Whelan and Gillespie helped Rangers draw 2-2.

From here on Liverpool were superb in the Championship. As Chelsea fell away and West Ham faced fixture congestion, the Reds assumed the winning habit, and waited for Everton to drop points.

Everton obliged. As both the Merseyside giants fought through to the FA Cup Final – Liverpool with a 2-0 victory over Southampton – it was apparent that either could perform the coveted Double.

On 16 April Liverpool at last assumed the League leadership on goal difference, but Everton retained a game in hand. On 26 April Everton drew at Forest and on 30 April lost at Oxford. Liverpool meanwhile were piling up the goals in big wins.

On 3 May they arrived at Stamford Bridge for their last game, needing a win to be sure of the title. The ground was full and the crowd saw Liverpool triumphant as Dalglish himself scored the only goal of the match, taking the ball on his chest before volleying sweetly across the goalkeeper into the far corner of the net. The Reds had led the Championship for only 17 days, but were on top on the day that mattered. Dalglish, in his first season as player-manager, had re-established Liverpool as the best side in the country.

Oddly, partly because of injuries and Dalglish's practice of flitting into and out of the team, the very best side was still not certain. Perhaps Liverpool's strength was in the team spirit of the squad. The players who contributed significantly were Grobbelaar, Neal, Kennedy, Nicol, Beglin, Gillespie, Lee, Lawrenson, Hansen, Molby, Dalglish, Whelan, MacDonald, Johnston, Rush, Wark, Walsh and McMahon.

On 10 May, Everton were the FA Cup Final opponents at Wembley, and, as described later, the Reds came from behind for an emphatic victory. The Double was only the fifth ever achieved in almost 100 years of League football, and it set the seal on the most successful decade any English club has ever had. What next for these Super-Reds?

The triumphant Liverpool team at Wembley after winning the 1986 FA Cup, and the Double

Famous Reds

This chapter contains biographies of 44 players who have helped make Liverpool the greatest soccer power in Britain. They range from Billy Liddell, Liverpool's greatest player of the years following the Second World War, through the players who helped Shankly put Liverpool on the soccer map, to Jan Molby, the Dane who established himself in the 1985-86 season.

Jim Beglin

Jim Beglin, like Ronnie Whelan, comes from the Republic of Ireland, and with team-mates Whelan and Lawrenson is in the national side. He was born in Waterford on 29 July 1963 and soon showed his skill at football. He was signed by Shamrock Rovers, from whom Liverpool obtained his transfer in May 1983. He made his debut against Southampton in November 1984, and was in the possession of the left-back spot at the end of the season, playing in the European Cup Final which ended so tragically in Brussels. In the 1985-86 season he took over from Alan Kennedy and made the position his own, winning Championship and Cup medals as the Reds performed the Double.

Gerry Byrne

Gerry Byrne was a one-club man, born in Liverpool on 29 March 1938, signing as a junior in 1955, and remaining on the books as a player until 1968. A full back, he made 273 League appearances for the club. He was in the side which brought Liverpool back to the First Division in 1961-62 and shared in the Championship years of 1963-64 and 1965-66. He was a hero in the winning Cup Final side of 1965, playing for 107 minutes of the game in those pre-substitute days with a broken collar bone. He won two England caps, and was in the final squad of 22 for the 1966 World Cup. Knee problems ended his career, and he joined the Liverpool staff.

Gerry Byrne, Cup Final hero of 1956.

Ian Callaghan

In the distant past of 1963-64, when Liverpool were winning only their sixth ever League Championship, Ian Callaghan, a brilliant winger, played in every League match of the season. In 1977 when Liverpool at last won the European Cup, Ian Callaghan, slightly slower perhaps, was a constructive

Ian Callaghan, OBE, long-serving winger and mid-field maestro.

midfield player in the Final, having taken his total of League appearances past 600.

Callaghan was born in Liverpool, on 10 April 1942, and signed on for Bill Shankly for the usual fee of £10, surely one of the best signings even Shankly ever made. Six days after his 18th birthday he made his debut against Bristol Rovers in the Second Division. He was a fast non-stop busy winger, making many goals with accurate crosses, and, when he became established, scoring about five a season himself. He became an Under-23 international, and won two fulls caps in 1966, one against France during England's triumphant progress through the World Cup finals. Thereafter, he was ignored by Alf Ramsey, who was not keen on wingers.

He missed some matches in the 1970-71 season after a cartilage operation, but resumed as an automatic choice next season in mid-field.

In his early days he had been moved from wing-half to the wing because at 5 ft 7 in (1·70 m) he was considered too small for mid-field. Although he was supposedly in the twilight of his career, Shankly considered 1971-72 his finest season, and in 1974 he was the football writers' Footballer of the Year. By then he had three Championship medals, two FA Cup winners medals and a UEFA Cup winners medal, but if this were a sentimental award for a whole-hearted one-club man, the journalists were mistaken, for even better was to come.

In 1977 came the European Cup win, and later Ron Greenwood picked the 35-year-old for two more England caps. He had shared in all Liverpool's great successes to 1977, but early in 1978 he finally lost his place in the side, and sat on the bench as Liverpool retained the European Cup. He was given a free transfer and joined his old colleague John Toshack, then managing Swansea. After helping Swansea into the Second Division, he went to Cork United, and then to Soudifjord in Norway. But in his 19 seasons at

Liverpool he had established a record of 640 League appearances, was the only player to span the club's progress from the Second Division to the European Cup victory, and was a model sportsman on the field – a suitable recipient for the OBE he was awarded in 1976.

Jimmy Case

Jimmy Case was a popular Liverpool player who dealt the club a severe blow later when playing for Brighton.

He was born in Liverpool on 18 May 1954 and joined the Reds from South Liverpool in May 1973. He made his League debut in November 1974, and for the next three seasons was more often in the side than out, but could not command a regular place. This came in two seasons only, in 1978-79 and 1979-80. In 1980-81 he played 14 games and 10 as a substitute, and in August 1981 left for Brighton for £350,000.

Case was an old-fashioned type of inside forward with a very hard shot. He often took Liverpool's free-kicks. He was in four Championship winning sides, but was on the losing side in the 1977 FA Cup Final, although he scored with a typical savage drive. He played in both legs of the UEFA Cup Final of 1976, which Liverpool won, coming on as a substitute in one, and played in three European Cup Final wins, although he was taken off in 1978 and came on only as a substitute in 1981.

It was a good record, but not the last Anfield had seen of him, because he scored the winning goal by which Brighton eliminated Liverpool in the FA Cup in 1982-83.

Jimmy Case, scorer of many goals with his powerful shooting.

Ray Clemence

Before Keegan joined Liverpool from Scunthorpe, Ray Clemence had followed the same route. Born on 8 August 1948 in Skegness, he played four matches for Scunthorpe in 1965-66 and a full season the following year before being bought by Shankly for around £15,000. He understudied Tommy Lawrence for two seasons, finally making his first-team debut in 1969-70, and establishing a regular place the following season. After four Under-23 Caps, he played his first international against Wales in 1974, and for many years thereafter he and Peter Shilton shared the England jersey.

Another save from the dependable Ray Clemence.

Clemence is not a flashy goalkeeper. Positional sense and dependability are his virtues. He played his part in all Liverpool's triumphs through the 1970s, being one of five who played in the first three European Cup Finals. In 1978-79 he played in all 42 League matches and conceded only 16 goals, arguably the best defensive record in any season's football.

In August 1981, while still at the top of his profession, Clemence was transferred to Tottenham Hotspur for £300,000 and continued in excellent form, immediately winning another FA Cup winners medal and extending his England career, bringing his caps to 61 by the end of the 1985-86 season.

Peter Cormack

Peter Cormack was born in Edinburgh on 17 July 1946, and played nearly 200 games for Hibernian before joining Nottingham Forest in March 1970. He was impressive as a clever mid-field player and was signed by Liverpool in July 1972.

He played for Liverpool for 3½ seasons, initially as a mid-field attacker and later, more interestingly, as a constructive player wearing the number 5 shirt. He won a Championship medal in his first season and played in every League match in 1973-74, winning an FA Cup winners medal at the end of the season. He was also in the UEFA Cup winning side in 1972-73.

Peter Cormack, a constructive mid-fielder.

Cormack won nine caps for Scotland while with Hibs and Forest. Strangely, he did not win another while playing so well for Liverpool. Perhaps the Scots were unsure of his role in the number 5 shirt. In November 1976 he left Anfield to end his League days with Bristol City.

Kenny Dalglish

When Kevin Keegan left Liverpool for Continental riches in 1977, Bob Paisley realised that only the best possible replacement would suffice. Keegan had been the inspiration of Liverpool, and another player capable of directing the attack of the European Cup holders in the same manner would be hard to find. Paisley found the only player who, in hindsight, would be guaranteed to do the job. He bought Kenny Dalglish from Celtic, and Liverpool retained the European Cup and hardly faltered in their run of League successes. Dalglish played brilliantly from the start, and announced his donning of the Keegan mantle with a superb winning goal against Bruges in the 1978 European Cup Final.

Dalglish, born on 4 March 1951 in Glasgow, had already played 47 times for Scotland when Liverpool signed him, and had scored over 100 League goals for Celtic. His style perfectly complements the style of Liverpool as a whole. Whereas the team make progress with quick passes, Dalglish is the one player who likes holding the ball. He is a target man who collects the

ball on the ground and with his strong hips is able to twist and turn and shield the ball while colleagues run into scoring positions for a pass. He is also an excellent goal scorer himself. When he scored at Ipswich on 26 November 1983 he became the first player to score 100 goals for one club in both the Scottish and English Leagues – for Celtic and Liverpool. In 1985-86 he also became the first Scot to win 100 international caps.

After the Heysel Stadium tragedy in May 1985 Joe Fagan resigned as manager of Liverpool, and Dalglish was appointed in his place. He had recently signed a four-year contract as a player, and intended to continue playing, with Bob Paisley as a mangerial adviser. Less than a year later, he had become the first player-manager to lead his team out at Wembley in the FA Cup Final, and ended his first season by leading his team to the Double. He had six Championship medals, three European Cup medals, an FA Cup medal, four League/Milk Cup medals, six Scottish Championship medals (with Celtic) and four Scottish Cup medals.

Bruce Grobbelaar

Bruce Grobbelaar was born in South Africa on 6 October 1957, and entered League football via Vancouver Whitecaps. In 1979 he played 24 League games for Crewe Alexandra (and scored a goal) before going back to Vancouver. In March 1981 Liverpool signed him for £250,000 and surprised the soccer world by making him first-choice goalkeeper at the start of the 1981-82 season, replacing England's Ray Clemence with a comparatively unknown player.

Grobbelaar has known little but playing success with Liverpool, the team winning the Championship and Milk Cup in each of his first three years, and the European Cup coming in his third year. In 1985-86 came the League and FA Cup Double. Grobbelaar's athleticism, which leads to displays of handstands after victories as well as flying catches during them, and his sense of fun, such as his knobbly knees act during the penalty shoot-out in the 1984 European Cup Final, are found entertaining by most fans, but he is prone to spectacular error and has his critics. He is a footballer who is not afraid to enjoy the game on a sporting level. He has played international football for Zimbabwe and is good enough to be in line for a cap were he eligible for any of the major soccer nations.

Brian Hall

Brian Hall's career was always linked with Steve Heighway's simply because both had University degrees – Hall was a B.Sc from Liverpool University. Like Heighway, Hall was born out of England, despite having an English father. He was born on 22 November 1946 in Glasgow. He played for Lancashire Grammar Schools, had trials with Blackburn, Bolton and Preston, and finally was offered terms by Liverpool. He was three years in the reserves, made two first-team appearances in 1968-69, and became established in the side at the same time as Heighway, in 1970-71.

Brian Hall was short at 5 ft 6 in (1·67 m) but had tremendous energy and was a worker in mid-field. He played in both Liverpool's FA Cup Finals in the 1970s, taking one winners medal, and won Championship and UEFA Cup winners medals in 1972-73. Halfway through the 1975-76 season, when Liverpool repeated this double, Hall lost his place in the side to Jimmy Case, and in the close season he was transferred to Plymouth Argyle. A season later he went to Burnley, then continued his career in non-League football.

Alan Hansen

Scot Alan Hansen was born on 13 June 1955 in Alloa, and joined Liverpool for £100,000 from Partick Thistle in April 1977. He made his League debut in September the following season, playing 18 matches in 1977-78. Soon after the start of the 1978-79 season he had made the number 6 shirt his own, and has been a regular first choice ever since.

At 6 ft 1 in (1·85 m) and 13 stone (82·5 kg), he is a tall, elegant central defender, whose assets are positional sense, coolness and an awareness of when to move forward. His close control frequently allows him to surge upfield with the ball and create openings in the opposition goal area. He played for Liverpool in the 1978, 1981 and 1984 European Cup Final victories, and in the 1985 defeat in Brussels.

His first appearance for Scotland was in 1979. By the end of the 1985-86 season he had won over 20 caps, six First Division Championship medals, an FA Cup medal, one Scottish First Division medal (with Partick Thistle), one League Cup and two Milk Cup medals. With Lawrenson he forms the heart of the Liverpool defence, and he was captain in 1985-86 when the Double was achieved. It was a surprise and probably an injustice when he was omitted from the Scottish World Cup squad to Mexico in 1986.

Below *Tony Hateley, short-stay centre-forward.*
Bottom *Steve Heighway, flying winger.*

Tony Hateley

The wanderings of Tony Hateley in the 1960s were legendary. Born on 13 June 1941 in Derby, he signed for Notts County and had spells at Aston Villa and Chelsea before joining Liverpool in July 1967 for £96,000, then a big fee.

Hateley was a very tall centre-forward, who was brilliant with his head. He played 39 League games for Liverpool in 1967-68, scoring 16 goals, but Shankly clearly did not think he was the answer to Liverpool's needs, for after four games of the following season he left for Coventry City, Liverpool recouping £80,000 of the fee. Thereafter he played for Birmingham, before returning to Notts County, and then moving to Oldham. He scored over 200 League goals, at an average of a goal every two matches throughout his career.

Steve Heighway

Steve Heighway was born on 25 November 1947 in Dublin, where his British father was working. He did not play or see a game of soccer until the family moved back to England when he was 10 years old. He watched Sheffield United, played for Skelmersdale United as an amateur, and at 23 was signed by Liverpool. He immediately attracted attention for a number of reasons. First, he and another Liverpool newcomer, Brian Hall, were graduates, Heighway having gained a degree in economics from Warwick University. These two players were taken as proof that the abolition of the maximum wage, which happened in 1961, now made football an attractive career for the educated young man. Secondly, Heighway chose to play for the Republic of Ireland – and made his first international appearance before he played for Liverpool. Thirdly, he went straight into Liverpool's first team, and proved a matchwinner with his electrifying dashes down the wing, stepping over the legs of tacklers and swerving inside and out at will.

Heighway scored in the FA Cup Final in his first season, 1970-71, but Arsenal scored twice. However, two seasons later he won a Championship medal and a UEFA Cup winners medal, and in 1974 he scored in the Cup

Final again, this time being on the winning side. He set up two goals in the first European Cup win in 1977 and came on as a substitute to win his second medal the following year.

By this time Heighway frequently wore the number 9 shirt, but operated more on the wings than down the centre. His era was exactly the 1970s because in 1979-80 most of his appearances were as a substitute. Younger men were taking over, and his contract was cancelled in April 1981, after 331 League appearances. He went to play for Minnesota Kicks in the USA, and continued to play for the Republic of Ireland, taking his total caps to 33.

Emlyn Hughes

Emlyn Hughes might have become a player more at home with an oval ball than a spherical one, because his father was a Rugby League player. Moreover, he was born in Barrow-in-Furness, Rugby League territory, and his parents were Welsh. Emlyn did, indeed, try rugby, but found he was better at soccer.

He was born on 28 August 1947, and was signed by Blackpool in 1964 as a junior. He was spotted by Bill Shankly and Liverpool paid £65,000 for his signature in March 1967. He was one of Shankly's best buys in his rebuilding programme. Hughes proved himself an adaptable player, equally at home at full-back, centre back or in mid-field.

His tremendous enthusiasm, and the way he flung himself all around the park earned him the nickname of 'Crazy Horse', and eventually the Liverpool captaincy. Hughes won almost all the honours in the game with Liverpool, and was captain when Liverpool first took the European Cup in 1977.

Following pages Alan Hansen, elegant central defender, gets up to beat Paul Goddard of West Ham.

Emlyn Hughes, a fine all-rounder, who captained both Liverpool and England in the 1970s.

Despite his Welsh parentage, Hughes chose to play for England, and made his debut against Wales in 1970. His usual position became left back, although evidence suggested that his left foot was less reliable than his right. He became the England captain, and despite being out of favour for a while when Revie was manager, returned to continue his international career until 1980, when he made his last three appearances, two as a substitute while a Wolverhampton player. In all he won 62 caps.

Hughes was fast and strong, making up for a slight lack of finesse with tremendous energy. He finally left Liverpool in 1979, after 474 League appearances and well over 500 senior games. He joined Wolves for a couple of seasons, then Rotherham as player-manager, then did a few months at Hull, looked in at Mansfield and finally in 1983 joined the Liverpool Old Boys Club at Swansea. His infectious personality gained him a regular spot (as captain again) in BBC TV's popular quiz 'A Question of Sport'.

Roger Hunt

Roger Hunt, Liverpool's top scorer.

From the time when Roger Hunt came into the Liverpool side in 1959-60 he was one of the club's leading goal scorers. In his first season he notched 21 League goals, and in his third, his best, he scored 41 from 41 games.

He was born on 20 July 1938, and came into the Second Division Liverpool side aged 21, after his National Service and just before Shankly took over. He was big, strong, hard running and determined, always looking for goals and rarely missing the chance to score. In the season in which he scored 41 he was chosen for England, and scored against Austria. He played in all the matches in the 1966 World Cup finals, and Ramsey chose him and Hurst to spearhead the attack in the Final itself, despite Greaves being fit, a fact which causes resentment among Greaves fans to this day. Unhappily, this affected Hunt, who, as he said, could never play like Greaves, and just wanted to do the job the manager picked him for.

Hunt was not a natural, and did not find the game easy. In 1969 he found the pressure of maintaining his goal ratio was getting to him and asked Ramsey not to consider him. In 1969-70 he was dropped by Liverpool after ten seasons of being an automatic choice, and later in the season was transferred to Bolton Wanderers, for whom he played another two and a half seasons. He played 402 League games for Liverpool and scored 245 goals, the club record. He won two Championship medals, an FA Cup winners medal, and, of course, a World Cup winners medal, and of his 34 games for England, only two were lost.

David Johnson

David Johnson is one of those players who wore both the red of Liverpool and the blue of Everton. Born in Liverpool on 23 October 1951 he signed as an apprentice for Everton in 1969. After 11 goals in 50 League appearances, he went to Ipswich in November 1972, where he was capped for England at centre forward before joining Liverpool in August 1976. He was on the books until August 1982, during which time he made 128 League appearances plus 21 as a substitute, only looking reasonably certain of his place for about three seasons from 1978-79. He did play in the European Cup Final in 1981, however.

In 1982 Johnson returned to Everton. He won eight England caps, three in 1975 and five in 1980.

Craig Johnston

Craig Johnston arrived at Anfield by a circuitous route. He was born in Johannesburg, South Africa, on 8 December 1960 and played in Australia for Lake McQuarrie and Sydney City before coming to England to join Middlesbrough in February 1978. His exciting style attracted the attention of Liverpool, and he joined the Reds in April 1981, getting a run in the first team towards the end of the 1981-82 season. He was frequently in and out of the side, but really blossomed in the Double year of 1985-86, when he established himself in the side and played well.

Johnston is a very strong player who is difficult to shake off the ball, often setting up chances by beating defenders for speed down the touchlines. He has collected a European Cup medal, three Championship medals, an FA Cup medal and two Milk Cup medals. He played twice for England Under-21s.

Joey Jones

Joey Jones was born in Llandudno on 4 March 1955 and joined Liverpool in July 1975 after 98 League games for Wrexham. He was at Anfield for three years, making 72 League appearances. They were important years for Liverpool, and Jones was a belligerent left back in the run of success.

In 1975-76, a Championship year, Jones lost his left-back place half-way through the season to Smith. He was a regular in 1976-77, another Championship year, and played in the European Cup Final victory. In 1977-78, he again lost his place half-way through the season, and in October 1978 he returned to Wrexham, later moving to Chelsea.

Jones won 18 Welsh caps with Liverpool, and had taken his total to 53 by the end of the 1982-83 season.

Top Craig Johnston, fast strong raider.
Above Joey Jones celebrates another triumph.

Kevin Keegan

When Bill Shankly bought Kevin Keegan for £35,000 on 1 May 1971, a week before Liverpool lost the FA Cup Final, he made one of football's best bargains. Keegan, born on 15 February 1951, signed schoolboy forms for Coventry but had drifted into Sunday football before Scunthorpe United put him into their Fourth Division side in 1968-69. Three seasons and 18 League goals later, he was playing for Liverpool and with his speed, courage, skill and goal-getting ability he was the immediate favourite of the Kop. He was a complete footballer, even being dangerous in the air, despite being only 5 ft 8 in (1·73 m).

Keegan was the tireless, all-action charismatic player who completed the successful side built by Shankly. He was outstanding in the FA Cup Final in 1974, and in the Championship and UEFA Cup double of 1975-76. The following season he again produced one of his best games in the European Cup Final, and captained England throughout the season.

During 1976-77 Keegan decided that he wanted to play on the Continent. During his six years with Liverpool he had won three Championship medals (two seconds and a third in the other years), two UEFA Cup medals, a European Cup medal and an FA Cup medal. SV Hamburg won his signature for £500,000. He continued to play for England, was a great success for Hamburg and was voted European Footballer of the Year in 1978 and 1979. He then came back to England to play for Southampton, and after a couple of seasons went to Newcastle United.

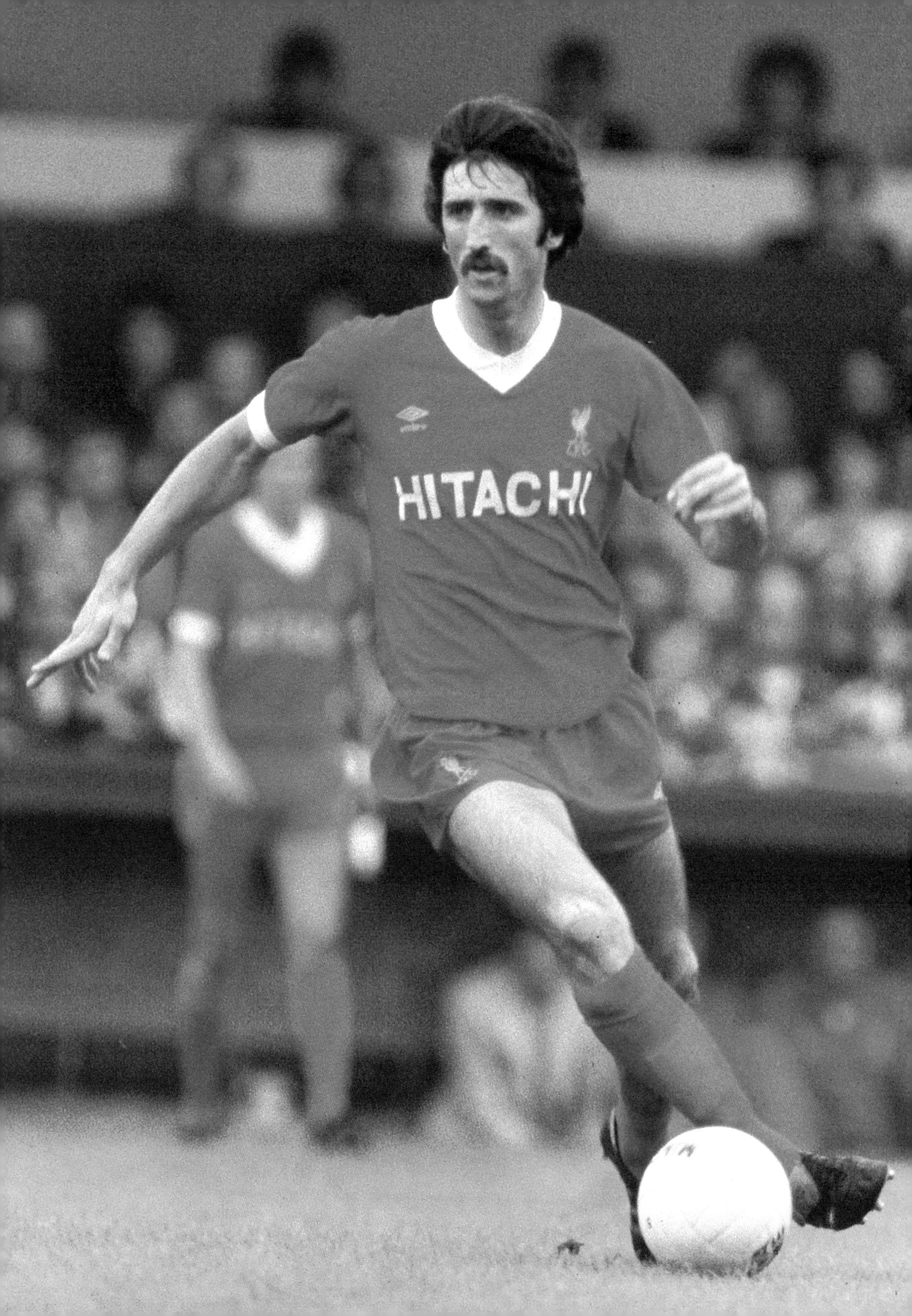
HITACHI

Injury meant Keegan appeared only as a substitute in England's last match in the 1982 World Cup finals, and he was not chosen when Bobby Robson took over the national team management. He had played 63 times for his country.

Above *Keegan leaps highest and heads towards goal.*
Opposite *David Johnson played for both top Merseyside clubs.*

Alan Kennedy

Alan Kennedy is one of two Newcastle United players who played against Liverpool in the 1974 FA Cup Final and who were later signed by the Reds. While McDermott was bought almost immediately Liverpool waited four years for Kennedy, finally paying £300,000 for him in August 1978.

Kennedy was born in Sunderland on 31 August 1954. A fast left-back he went straight into the side in the 1978-79 season, filling a gap left by Joey Jones the season before. He mixes his defensive game with charges down the left touchline, frequently getting in powerful shots, some of which end in the net. Twice he has scored vital European Cup Final goals. In 1981 he scored the only goal eight minutes from the end and in 1984 he netted the fourth and vital penalty which brought Liverpool victory in the shoot-out. He was called up for his first cap for England in 1984, when nearly 30. He began the 1985-86 season in the first team, but lost his place early on to Jim Beglin.

Ray Kennedy

In 1971 Ray Kennedy scored two minutes from the end of Arsenal's last League match with Spurs to clinch the Championship, and five days later helped Arsenal beat Liverpool in the FA Cup Final to record the fourth and last 'double'. On 20 July 1974 he became a Liverpool player for £180,000.

Born on 28 July 1951, he was signed as an apprentice by Arsenal and made his debut aged 19 in 1970. He was a free-scoring inside forward, and Arsenal's top scorer in his first season. After about a season and a half Liverpool converted him to a powerhouse mid-field player. A burly 5 ft 11 in (1·80 m) he developed the strength to win the ball and distribute it to good effect, and did not lose his ability to come forward and score with powerful shots. One of his most valuable goals for Liverpool was in the 1980-81 European Cup semi-final at Bayern Munich which set up a 1-1 draw after Liverpool had been held 0-0 at Anfield.

Kennedy played in all three of Liverpool's European Cup Final victories, and his collection of medals with Arsenal and Liverpool is astonishing: three other European medals, three Championships, two FA Cup medals. He played 17 times for England. In January 1982 he was transferred to Swansea for £160,000. He made 258 League appearances for Liverpool.

Chris Lawler

Chris Lawler was a long-serving full-back for Liverpool, who had the happy knack of scoring vital goals. He was born in Liverpool on 20 October 1943 and joined the club as a junior in 1960, making his first team debut in 1962. He made 406 League appearances for the Reds and scored 41 goals before he left for Portsmouth (manager: Ian St John) in October 1975. His career at Liverpool, therefore, more or less coincided with Shankly's managership, and he shared in all the honours. There were three Championships, an FA Cup Winners medal in 1965 and the UEFA Cup win in 1972-73. He played four times for England. After a couple of seasons with Portsmouth, he ended his League career in 1977-78 at Stockport County. He currently coaches Liverpool reserves.

Chris Lawler, scoring full-back.

Tommy Lawrence

Goalkeeper Tommy Lawrence was on Liverpool's books for 14 years, signing in November 1957 from the juniors and leaving for Tranmere in September 1971 after 306 League matches. He was born on 14 May 1940 in Dailly, West Scotland.

Lawrence made his League debut in the 1962-63 season. Liverpool had been promoted from the Second Division the season before, and Lawrence took over from Jim Furnell in October 1962. In 1963-64 Liverpool were Champions and in 1965 Lawrence added a Cup winners medal to his honours. There was another Championship the following season. His first European venture ended when Inter Milan erased a 3-1 Anfield deficit by winning 3-0 in Milan, the vital goal coming when Lawrence had the ball kicked from his hands in a controversial manner.

Lawrence lost his first-team place to Clemence in 1970, when, strangely, he was recalled for two more Scottish caps, having played once before for his country in 1963.

Tommy Lawrence, 1960s goalkeeper.

Following pages *Ray Kennedy battling his way through a bunch of opponents.*

Mark Lawrenson

Mark Lawrenson was born in Preston on 2 June 1957 and joined Preston North End as a junior. He was signed by Brighton in July 1977 and helped the team into the First Division before Liverpool paid £900,000 for his services in August 1981. He went straight into the first team, and has been practically a regular since, winning four Championship medals, an FA Cup medal and three Milk Cup medals, as well as a European Cup medal in 1984.

Lawrenson is a very fast defender with a strong tackle. He and Hansen in the centre of Liverpool's defence complement each other well – while Hansen often moves upfield, Lawrenson's speed enables him to cover in almost a sweeper's role.

He was capped by the Republic of Ireland in 1977 while only a 20-year-old at Preston, being eligible as his father is Irish, and has played regularly since for his chosen country. He was born in England, however, and had he wished to wait he would almost certainly be an automatic choice for England today.

Billy Liddell, Liverpool's most famous player of the immediate post-war years.

Sammy Lee

Sammy Lee is a Liverpudlian through and through. He was born in the city on 7 February 1959, and signed apprentice forms for the club in April 1976. He made his debut for the first team in the 1977-78 season, when he appeared twice as a substitute. Next season he played one full League match, and he did not claim a regular place in the side until 1980. His rise was rapid, and he became an essential part of the midfield powerhouse.

Lee does not look like a member of Europe's most successful club side. He is only 5 ft 7 in (1·70 m) and weighs just over 10 stone (64 kg), but he is well-muscled and chunky and gets through a lot of work on the right flank of both defence and attack. In 1983 he was picked for England and made a promising start in internationals.

Lee's aggression, enthusiasm and energy keep him always in the game, and in his first five seasons brought three Championship medals, four League and Milk Cup medals, two European Cup medals and 14 caps. He lost his place in the 1984-85 season, and, while remaining a valuable member of the squad, had difficulty in re-establishing a regular place.

Sammy Lee, mid-field dynamo, gets through to score.

Billy Liddell

Because of the Second World War, when he was an RAF navigator, Billy Liddell did not appear in Liverpool's first team until the 1946-47 season. He was then 24, having been born on 8 January 1922 in Dunfermline, Scotland. Liverpool beat Chelsea 7-4, and went on to win the Championship. This was the only honour Liddell won with Liverpool, apart from an FA Cup runners-up medal in 1950. Indeed Liverpool were relegated in 1954. But the pace, skill, directness and ferocious shooting of left-winger Liddell earned him the nickname 'King Billy'. He was so dominant that for a time Liverpool were known as 'Liddellpool'.

He played during the era of the £20 maximum wage, so became an accountant as well as a footballer, becoming bursar at Liverpool University (and incidentally a JP) after his retirement in 1961. In his 14 seasons he made a record number of League appearances for Liverpool (492) and scored a record number of League goals (216). Nearly half of these were from the wing – he switched to centre forward in 1954.

He won 28 caps for Scotland, and a measure of his greatness was that he and Stanley Matthews were the only players to appear in both Great Britain sides against the Rest of the World, in 1947 and 1955. He would have graced any of the European Cup sides of over 20 years later.

Following pages *Mark Lawrenson, the king-pin of the central defence in the 1980s.*

Alec Lindsay

Alec Lindsay was the regular left-back in the Liverpool side for several seasons between 1969 and 1976. Born in Bury on 27 February 1948 he left Bury for Liverpool in March 1969. He played 21 times in 1970-71 and was thereafter unchallenged until the middle of the 1974-75 season, when Phil Neal took over.

Lindsay was a fair-haired mobile player who formed with Lawler a pair of attacking full backs. His most successful year was 1972-73 when Liverpool won the Championship and the UEFA Cup, and he was a vital member of the side. He won an FA Cup winners medal in 1974. In 1977, after 168 League games for Liverpool, he was transferred to Stoke City. He won four caps for England.

Below *Alec Lindsay, mobile left-back.*
Bottom *Larry Lloyd, towering centre-half.*

Larry Lloyd

Larry Lloyd was the big Liverpool centre-half of the early 1970s. He was born in Bristol on 6 October 1948 and signed as a junior for Bristol Rovers. He joined Liverpool in April 1969.

At 6 ft 2 in (1·88 m) and approaching 13 stone (82·5 kg) Lloyd was tall and commanding, winning most of the balls in the air and generally being a strong man in a defence which included Lawler, Lindsay and Smith. He was in the Championship winning side of 1972-73. In August 1974 he left Liverpool for Coventry, and subsequently played for Nottingham Forest and Wigan, winning both Championship and European Cup medals while at Forest. He won three England caps in 1971 and 1972 while with Liverpool and another in 1980 while with Forest, when recalled for a match against Wales.

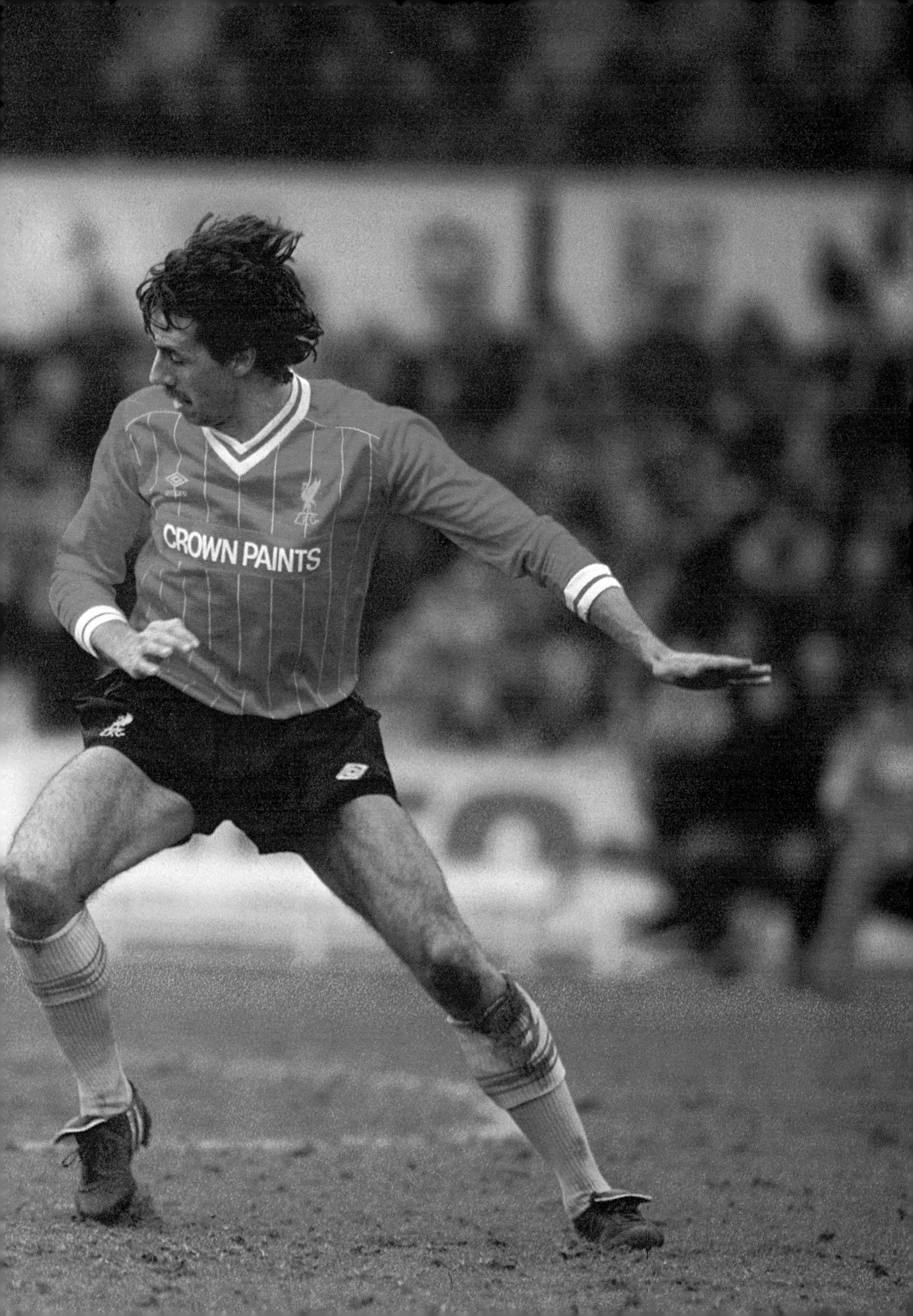
CROWN PAINTS

Terry McDermott

Terry McDermott was born on 8 December 1951 in Kirby, and signed as an apprentice for Rochdale in 1969. He was a wing-half, and impressed Newcastle, who bought him in 1973. McDermott spent two seasons with the Geordies and played well against Liverpool in the 1974 FA Cup Final, although Newcastle were the losing side. Liverpool signed him in November 1974.

McDermott developed into a clever midfield player who scored some outstanding goals. He returned to Wembley with the Reds in 1977, but was again on the losing side. However, he shared in all the triumphs of the late 1970s and early 1980s, being in the European Cup winning team in 1977, 1978 and 1981. In that first victory, he set the Reds on their way with the first goal. He was first picked for England in 1978 and won his 25th cap in 1982. After 221 League games for Liverpool, he returned to Newcastle in September 1982, where he and another former Anfield favourite, Kevin Keegan, spearheaded Newcastle's drive back towards the First Division. He was voted Footballer of the Year in 1980.

Terry McDermott, a useful midfield player for Liverpool in the late 1970s and early 1980s.

Gordon Milne

Gordon Milne was a small, cultured wing-half, who provided much of the craft in Shankly's first great side of the mid-1960s. He was born on 29 March 1937 in Preston, and joined Preston North End from non-League Morecambe in January 1956. He was transferred to Liverpool in September 1960, one of Shankly's early signings.

Milne played in all Liverpool's matches when promotion was won to the First Division in 1961-62, and won Championship medals in 1963-64 and 1965-66. He was unlucky in 1965, however, when injury ruled him out of the side which won the FA Cup at Wembley. He left Liverpool in May 1967 to finish his career at Blackpool.

Milne played 14 times for England, all while at Liverpool. He was in the 27 for the 1966 World Cup training, but was one of the five left out of the final squad.

Gordon Milne was one of the best players in Shankley's first great side in the mid-1960s.

Kevin MacDonald

Kevin MacDonald was an early present for his mother, being born in Inverness three days before Christmas Day, 1960. He was brought into the English League by Leicester City, who bought him from Inverness Caley in 1979. He made his first full League appearance in December 1980 wearing a No 11 shirt, but settled down as a right-sided midfield player. After 152 first-team appearances he joined Liverpool for £400,000 in November 1984. He made his debut on 29 December 1984 against Luton, and during a run of a dozen games was regarded as a possible midfield 'engine-room' successor to Graeme Souness. He subsequently found difficulty getting into the side, however, and was frequently on the substitute bench in 1985-86, although he made the Wembley side to win an FA Cup winners medal.

Jan Molby

Born in Kolding, on the Jutland peninsula, Denmark, on 4 July 1963, Jan Molby learned his football under the Danish national coaching scheme, and at 18 left for Amsterdam to cash in by playing for Ajax with his countryman Jesper Olsen. In the summer of 1984 they both came to Lancashire, and Molby went straight into the Liverpool side, wearing Souness's old shirt. However, the big Danish international, who looks overweight at around 14 stones, lost his place after 17 games to fellow newcomer MacDonald, and began to fear for his future at the club. He need not have worried. In 1985-86 he was a revelation, becoming Liverpool's midfield inspiration and a central defender if required. He was an essential part of the Double-winning side, winning his first English honours, and becoming a favourite of the Kop. He soon spoke English with a pronounced scouse accent. He likes Liverpool and Liverpool likes him, and he could be a Super-Red for a long time.

Jan Molby, the big Danish international, was the midfield inspiration in the successful Double-winning 1985–86 side.

Phil Neal

Neal was one of the more unsung heroes of Liverpool's run of triumph in the 1970s and 1980s. He was born in Irchester, Northants, on 20 February 1951 and joined Northampton Town in December 1968, playing for them for six seasons, for most of the time in the lower regions of the Fourth Division. He was an early signing by Bob Paisley, and soon earned a regular place in Liverpool's first team. In 1975-76 he took over from Keegan as the penalty taker, and scored two in a 2-2 draw with Arsenal at Anfield. By the end of the season he had scored six goals, five of them penalties. Next season he scored twelve penalties, two in a European Cup semi-final and one in the final, when his late penalty sealed a 3-1 victory for the Reds.

With Neal's arrival Liverpool did not have to worry about the right-back position. He was unspectacular but sound. If he had a weakness it was to be beaten for speed by a fast-running winger, but he compensated for this by excellent positional play. He also became an essential part of Liverpool's attack with his intelligent moves upfield in support of right-wing moves. He sometimes popped up unexpectedly in the penalty box and did not rely wholly on penalties for his goals – he scored in the 1984 European Cup Final.

Phil Neal was the backbone of Liverpool's defence from the mid-1970s to the end of 1985.

Neal was made club captain in 1984-85, ironically the first season for 10 years in which Liverpool failed to win a trophy. He himself is loaded with medals, no less than seven Championship medals, one League Cup and three Milk Cup medals, four European Cup medals (the only Liverpool player to appear in all four winning finals) and one Super Cup medal. He chalked up a half-century of England caps, appearing twice in the World Cup finals in 1982. He was approaching the end of his career when captaining Liverpool in the tragic European Cup Final of 1985. He began the victorious 1985-86 season at right-back, but lost his place half-way through the season to Steve Nicol, and in December 1985 left to become player/manager of Bolton Wanderers.

Steve Nicol

Steve Nicol was born in Irvine, Scotland, on 11 Dec. 1961, and signed for Ayr United. He did well, making 71 appearances before being signed by Liverpool for £300,000 in October 1981. He made his debut in August 1982, but did not get a run in the side until near the end of 1983. Never one of the 'glamorous' players, he established a place as a sound midfielder who scored occasional goals in the 1984-85 season. In 1985-86, the Double year, he appeared with a very short haircut and established himself as a regular, eventually taking over at right-back from Phil Neal. He won his second Championship medal and an FA Cup medal. He won a European Cup medal in 1984. An Under-21 international, he established himself in the Scottish side, and was picked in the World Cup squad for Mexico in 1986.

Steve Nicol in action against Watford.

Ian Rush

Although he did not join Liverpool until the 1980s Ian Rush has already established himself as the most dangerous goal-scorer in British football. He was born in St Asaph, North Wales, on 20 October 1961 and signed as an

apprentice with Chester in 1979. After 33 Third Division games and 14 goals he joined Liverpool in April 1980. In May he made his debut for Wales before he had appeared in a League match for Liverpool. It was not until the end of the 1980-81 season that he established a place at centre-forward.

Rush's goal-scoring feats began in 1981-82, when he appeared in 32 League games and was top scorer with 17, adding 11 more in the FA and League Cups. In 1982-83 he scored 24 League goals, and in 1983-84 began scoring even more freely, finishing the season with a total of 49 goals. At the same time he became an automatic choice for Wales. In 1985-86 he was outstanding in the Cup Final, when he scored twice to maintain a remarkable statistical curiosity – in 120 games in which he'd scored for Liverpool he had not been on a losing side. He now has four Championship medals, a European Cup medal, an FA Cup medal and four League/Milk Cup medals.

Rush is not the old-style battering-ram leader, or the tall target man like Toshack. He is more like Jackie Milburn, extremely fast off the mark and a deadly finisher when he has a sight of goal. He is slim and mobile, always aware of his position in relation to the goal and alert to ricochets and rebounds in the area. He is the deadliest finisher in the League since Greaves, and attracted foreign interest, eventually signing for Juventus in 1986, a deal that brought Liverpool £3.3 million, a record fee for a British player.

Ian St John, cultured attacker.

Ian St John

A famous Liverpool joke concerned a poster displayed in the town: 'What will you do when Christ comes to Liverpool?' to which a fan had added 'Move St John to inside right.'

Ian St John, born on 7 March 1938 in Motherwell, was a centre forward when he was signed by Shankly from his home club in May 1961, at £35,000 Liverpool's record buy. At only 5 ft 7½ in (1·71 m) he was later converted to an inside forward. He scored a hat-trick on his debut in the Liverpool Senior Cup (against Everton) and from 1961 onwards was a regular for nearly nine seasons. With good control on the ground, and an excellent header, he was always in the thick of the attack, and suffered numerous injuries which rarely prevented him playing – only in 1964-65 did he miss many games. That season he came back with his best moment – the superb header which won Liverpool the FA Cup in extra time. He also helped Liverpool win the Second Division in his first season, and later two Championships.

St John began his international career while at Motherwell, and made 21 appearances for Scotland, scoring nine goals. When Liverpool released him in 1971 he had made 335 League appearances, in which he scored 95 goals. He played in South Africa, but meanwhile reached the finals of a BBC TV contest to find a commentator for the Mexico World Cup, and he is now a regular opinionator on Independent Television.

Tommy Smith

Tommy Smith was born a few hundred yards from Anfield in April 1945 and signed as a professional for the club on his 17th birthday. He was brought up in a tough area and his football was soon noted for its toughness. He played one match in 1962-63 (Liverpool beat Birmingham 5-1 in their first season back in the First Division), but then waited two years for his next chance. This time he became a regular, and was soon the club captain.

He won an FA Cup medal in only his 38th appearance in 1965, and a Championship medal the following year, but in the 1970s honours came thick and fast. After ten England Under-23 appearances between 1965 and 1968, he won his only cap, against Wales, in 1971, in a match where his team-mates Lawler, Lloyd and Hughes joined him in the defence.

In 1972-73 he won another Championship medal (he ended with five), and the first of two UEFA Cup winners medals, and the following year won his second FA Cup winners medal. By now most of Smith's games were at right back, and when Neal moved across from the left he lost his regular place in the side. Injury to Phil Thompson, however, allowed Smith to gain a place in the latter half of the 1976-77 season, and he was in the side for the European Cup Final. This was his finest moment, as his thrilling headed goal from Heighway's corner restored Liverpool's lead and killed off Borussia's fight-back.

Smith had announced that this would be his last game, but his uncharacteristic goal persuaded him to go on. He made 22 more League appearances next season, but then moved on to Swansea City managed by his old colleague John Toshack. A hard tackle on Ossie Ardiles, playing his first season for Spurs, did not endear him to the critics, but showed Smith to be as uncomplicated and uncompromising as ever he was in his 467 League appearances for Liverpool.

Tommy Smith and trophies.

Graeme Souness, an inspiring captain in the 1980s.

Graeme Souness

Graeme Souness joined Liverpool from Middlesbrough in January 1978, soon after the arrival of Dalglish. A strong attacking wing-half, he had already won three caps for Scotland and was regarded as a player for the future. A schoolboy international, he was impressive against England at White Hart Lane, and Spurs beat Celtic for his signature. But homesickness took him farther north to Ayresome Park in January 1973.

Souness was born on 6 March 1953 in Edinburgh, and signed apprentice forms with Spurs when 17 years old. Liverpool paid Middlesbrough just over £350,000 for him, and he was quickly into the side, winning a European Cup winners medal in his first season of 1977-78, when it was his pass which allowed Dalglish to score the only goal in the final.

Souness took over the centre of the mid-field for Liverpool. At 5 ft 11 in (1·80 m), and weighing nearly 13 stone (82·5 kg) he is very strong in the tackle, sometimes accused of being a little too robust. But he is also a delicate ball-player and accurate passer, who brings a touch of arrogance to his game. He is a winner, and makes a crunching tackle or perceptive cross with the same intensity. As Liverpool's captain in the early 1980s he devoted his whole efforts to the cause, and with the possible exception of Dalglish was the most influential player in the team's make-up.

After three matches for Scotland in 1975, Souness became a regular in the national side after joining Liverpool in 1978, and by the end of the 1984-85 season his number of caps approached 50. His strength, control and a hard shot brought many successes and vital goals to Liverpool, including the winner in the 1984 Milk Cup Final.

He managed to acquire a grand total of five Championship medals, four League and Milk Cup medals and three European Cup medals with the Reds before, at the end of the 1983-84 season, he finally departed to Italy to play for Sampdoria, having made over 350 appearances for Liverpool. In 1986 he was appointed player-manager of Glasgow Rangers.

Peter Thompson, tricky winger.

Peter Thompson

Peter Thompson was what is now called 'an old-fashioned' winger. He was an artist, a player with great ball control who would make rapid progress down the left wing, beat his man and deliver the perfect cross.

He was born on 17 November 1942 in Carlisle and made his debut for Preston North End in 1960-61. After three seasons when he missed only four League matches, he was signed by Shankly for £35,000 and missed few games throughout the 1960s. He won four Under-23 caps in his first season at Liverpool (he had also won schoolboy and youth caps) and later in the season earned a regular place in the England team. On the American tour of 1964, he was hailed in Brazil and Argentina as the natural successor to Finney and Matthews. But Alf Ramsey evolved a style in which wingers were not wanted, and Thompson did not win the caps he might have done in another era. In both 1966 and 1970 he was in the initial World Cup selection, but dropped when the final squad of 22 was chosen. In all he played 16 times for England.

In the 1970s his appearances for Liverpool became less regular, and in January 1974 he was transferred to Bolton Wanderers, for whom he continued to play till 1978. He made 322 League appearances for Liverpool, winning two Championship and an FA Cup winners medal.

Phil Thompson

Phil Thompson is a son of Liverpool, born there on 21 January 1954 and looking no further than Anfield when he signed apprentice forms. He became a professional in February 1971, and appeared in the League as a substitute in 1971-72. He made 14 appearances the following season before becoming a regular in 1973-74. He played on the right-hand side of the defence, finally settling down as one of the centre backs, initially with Hughes. He played brilliantly in the 3-0 defeat of Newcastle in the 1974 FA Cup Final, but was so little known that security men tried to prevent him receiving his medal as he had swopped his shirt for a Newcastle one.

He soon established himself as the reliable last line of Liverpool's defence, eventually taking over as captain. In 1976 he was first chosen for England and performed his Liverpool act by becoming the steady man in the centre of the defence. His international career continued to 1983, when he had won 42 caps.

Thompson missed Liverpool's first European Cup win through injury, but appeared in the victorious finals of 1978 and 1981, having already collected a UEFA Cup winners' medal. The arrival of Hansen and Lawrenson at Anfield saw this great servant's career at the club as a first-team regular come to an end in the 1982-83 season.

Phil Thompson, steady in defence.

John Toshack

John Toshack was born in Cardiff on 22 March 1949, signed for Cardiff City, and was already a Welsh international when transferred to Liverpool for £110,000 in November 1970, aged 21. At 6 ft (1·83 m) he was a central striker, mobile and accurate with his head, and the team's main target man through most of the 1970s. He struck up a profitable twin-striker partnership with Keegan, who joined the club a few months after him, the ball flicked from Toshack's head to Keegan's feet leading to many goals.

A Toshack goal in a Welsh draw at Wembley in 1974 cost England a place in the 1974 World Cup finals, but a serious thigh injury in 1975 threatened his career. He came back to win his second and third Championship medals to add to his 1974 FA Cup medal, but injury kept him out of Liverpool's side in both the FA Cup Final of 1977 and the following European Cup Final – his biggest disappointment, for which two UEFA Cup medals were small consolation.

In 1978 after 172 League appearances and 74 goals for Liverpool, he became player-manager of Swansea City, and persuaded old colleagues Tommy Smith, Ian Callaghan and Phil Boersma to join him there. He was immediately successful and took Swansea from the Fourth to the First Division. When he finally retired from playing, he had taken his number of Welsh caps to 40.

Paul Walsh

Paul Walsh joined Charlton Athletic as an apprentice and signed for them in October 1979 when he became seventeen. His busy play attracted Luton, who paid £400,000 for him in July 1982. He caught the attention of Bobby Robson and made his England debut in the tour of Australia in 1983. Liverpool paid £700,000 for him near the end of the 1983-84 season, and he made his debut the following season.

Born on 1 October 1962, Walsh is small at 5 ft 8 in (1·73 m) and 10 st 1 lb (64 kg), particularly for a central attacker. He likes the ball on the ground and achieves his success by quickness, dribbling, good control and an eye for a half-chance. His goals against Austria Vienna in the European Cup quarter-final established his popularity at Anfield. He has represented England at Youth and Under-21 level and by 1984-85 had five full caps, but injury and the evergreen Dalglish limited his appearances in 1985-86, and his future with the club became problematical.

John Wark

John Wark joined Liverpool in 1984 to provide punch in mid-field and an extra player likely to score goals. After a long and distinguished career with Ipswich, he found a first-team place immediately.

He was born on 4 August 1957 in Glasgow, and was an apprentice with Ipswich before making his debut in the 1974-75 season. By the end of the 1982-83 season he had appeared in 264 First Division matches and scored 89 goals. He won an FA Cup winners medal in 1978 and a UEFA Cup winners

John Wark, 1984 addition to the first team.

medal in 1980-81. During that European campaign Wark scored 14 of Ipswich's goals.

Wark is a powerful mid-field player with an eye for goal, and scores many opportunist goals with head and foot. He was first capped for Scotland in 1979, played in all the World Cup matches of 1982, and had won 29 caps by the end of the 1984-85 season.

He made his debut for Liverpool at Watford on 31 March 1984, scoring the first goal in a 2-0 win. He was a regular in 1984-85, but was hampered by injury in 1985-86 and could not command a place. It seemed he might leave for a less powerful club.

Ron Whelan

Ron Whelan is one of the young players to make his way into the Liverpool side in the 1980s. He was born in Dublin on 25 September 1961 and joined Liverpool from Home Farm in October 1979, making his League debut against Stoke City on 3 April 1981, when he scored on his only appearance in the 1980-81 season. Next season he played three games in October and was then a regular for the rest of the League programme.

A hardworking mid-field player, usually on the left, he has a talent for scoring vital goals. Indeed, his goal ratio at the end of the 1981-82 season would not disgrace a striker: he had 11 goals in 33 League appearances. He has performed particularly well in Milk Cup Finals, with two excellent goals against Spurs in 1982 and another to win the match against Manchester United in 1983. He was a regular in the Double season, and now has four Championship medals, a European Cup medal, an FA Cup medal and three Milk Cup medals, and has played regularly for the Republic of Ireland since 1981-82. He is a vital player for both club and country.

Ron Whelan, Milk Cup Final scorer.

Ron Yeats

Ron Yeats was just about the biggest of Liverpool's centre-halves. He stood 6 ft 2 in (1·88 m) and weighed 14 stone 5 lb (91·2 kg). He was born in Aberdeen on 15 November 1937 and joined Liverpool in July 1961 from Dundee United for £30,000. He was ten years with Liverpool, making 358 League appearances.

Needless to say, Yeats was a commanding figure, whom Paisley chose in his best-ever Liverpool side. Yeats was in the side which won promotion from the Second Division in 1961-62, and the Championship in 1963-64. In 1965 the FA Cup was won, and Yeats, as captain, stepped up to receive it. The next season, 1964-65, Liverpool were Champions again. This team of the middle 1960s was Shankly's first good side, and Yeats was the kingpin around which it was built. He won two caps for Scotland. In December 1971 Yeats left Liverpool for a couple of seasons as player-manager at Tranmere Rovers, the Reds' 'Nursery side'.

Ron Yeats, huge centre-half and captain of the Shankly era.

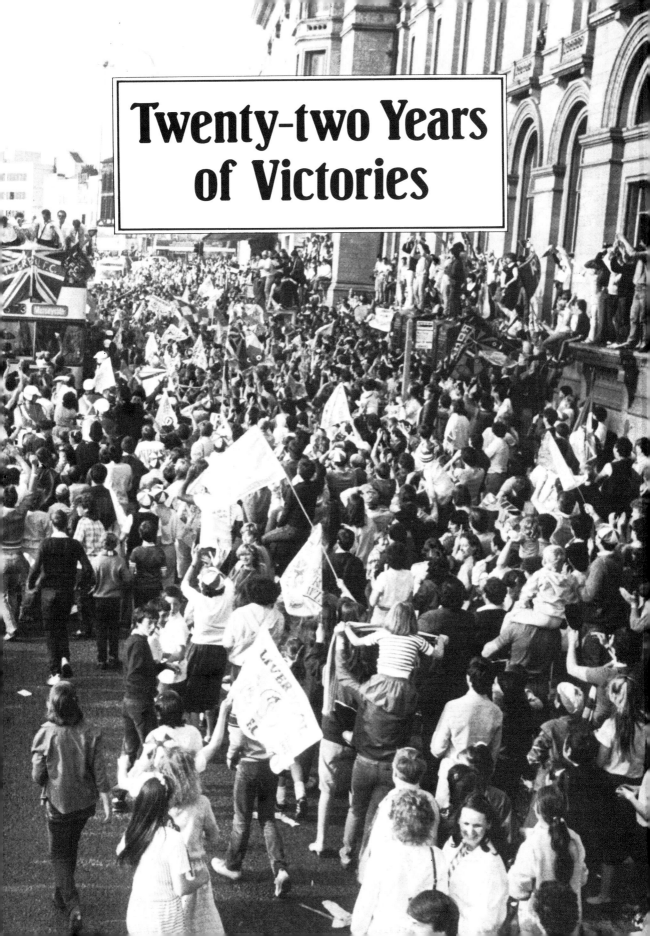

Twenty-two Years of Victories

Preceding pages *A not unusual scene in Liverpool. A triumphant homecoming after the 1984 European Cup win.*

Liverpool have registered many famous victories in the twenty years from the mid-1960s. This chapter gives accounts of some of the best, including the FA Cup Final wins, the European Cup wins, a significant League victory over old rivals Everton and two of the Football League Milk Cup triumphs.

FA Cup Final, 1965

Liverpool 2 Leeds United 1
after extra time

Liverpool were in the Cup Final for the first time since losing 2-0 to Arsenal in 1950. On a dull day the Koppites were present in force, singing 'Ey-aye-addio we're going to meet the Queen' before the kick-off. Liverpool were between Championship seasons, but had dropped to a disappointing seventh in the League, while Leeds, with an identical record to Manchester United, lost the title only on goal average.

Ron Yeats won the toss and chose the wind, and the opening minutes were marked by heavy tackling. Gerry Byrne, in fact, broke a collar-bone as early as the third minute. In those days there were no substitutes, and Byrne played on bravely to the end. Hunter and Bremner also needed attention and St John was cautioned by the referee. When it began to rain, many thought this was one of the least enjoyable finals for a long time. By half-time, neither goal had been seriously threatened; a hard Callaghan shot that hit and doubled up Charlton, before going for a corner, and a Smith shot just past the post being the nearest efforts.

A period of Liverpool pressure in driving rain after the interval came to nothing, but Liverpool always looked likeliest to score. Sprake saved well twice from Peter Thompson, once turning the ball for a corner at full stretch, then took the ball off Yeats' head in a dangerous position. In the conditions, both teams seemed tired when the whistle went with no score, and extra time was needed at Wembley for the first time for 18 years.

Everything changed three minutes after the restart. Thompson fed Gerry Byrne, overlapping on the left wing, Byrne turned the ball into the goalmouth and Roger Hunt, stooping low, headed home. The fans at last had something to cheer, but the goal brought out Leeds' fighting qualities, particularly those of Bremner and Charlton. Eight minutes after Hunt's goal, Charlton nodded down to Bremner, just inside the box and Bremner hit the dropping ball straight into the net for the equalizer.

In the final period of extra time, Bremner looked the most likely match-winner, but nine minutes from the end Ian Callaghan crossed hard from the right, and Ian St John rose to a ball which looked as if it might be just behind him and headed with great power into the net. Leeds tried to come back, but at the end it was Thompson testing Sprake again. Liverpool, in all-red, had beaten Leeds United, all-white, for their first-ever Cup win – it had taken 73 years.

Teams: *Liverpool:* Lawrence, Lawler, Byrne, Strong, Yeats, Stevenson, Callaghan, Hunt, St John, Smith, Thompson.
Leeds United: Sprake, Reaney, Bell, Bremner, Charlton, Hunter, Giles, Storrie, Peacock, Collins, Johanneson.

Opposite *Ian St John after scoring the winner in the 1965 FA Cup Final. Roger Hunt congratulates him.*

First Division match, 1970-71

Liverpool 3 Everton 2

When Liverpool returned to the First Division in 1962, Everton greeted the upstarts by becoming Champions. In the next seven seasons, each side was out of the first six only once, and when they met at Anfield on 21 November 1970, Everton were again Champions. Liverpool had been Champions twice in the meantime, and both sides had won the FA Cup. It was a period when to be the best of Merseyside was nearly as good as being Champions of the League.

Shankly had begun to rebuild Liverpool in the late 1960s, and Everton started favourites for this match. Three of England's 1970 World Cup squad were in the side: Alan Ball, Brian Labone and Tommy Wright. A fourth, Keith Newton, was substitute, having lost his place to new signing Henry Newton, from Nottingham Forest.

The first half went Everton's way, but there were no goals – thanks mainly to Ray Clemence's great save from Royle. Liverpool were slowly being outplayed, and eleven minutes into the second half, the inevitable goal came. Tommy Smith, Liverpool's captain, harassed by Johnny Morrissey, an ex-Liverpool player, played a ball across his own area straight to Alan Whittle, who chipped over the advancing Clemence. Eight minutes later Morrissey was away again down the left, centred, and Joe Royle put Everton two up. It seemed the Reds were sunk.

Keith Newton came on for Howard Kendall, and Phil Boersma replaced 18-year-old John McLaughlin. The tide was turned in the 69th minute, when Steve Heighway, in his first season, began one of those rapid runs cutting in from the left, and ended by placing a right-foot shot into the far corner. Suddenly the mixture of old and new players began to look like a side. Seven minutes later Heighway established himself as one of the new favourites of the Kop with more trickery on the left, ended by a centre which John Toshack, two weeks earlier a Cardiff player, headed in.

The Anfield faithful now wanted a winner, and it came eight minutes from the end, again from the left, when new boy Alec Lindsay floated the ball across, Toshack flicked it on, and old-stager Chris Lawler crashed it in. In the dying minutes Clemence played his part with another superb save, this time from Keith Newton.

Shankly expressed his pride in his new boys, while Liverpool again came from behind later in the season to beat Everton in the FA Cup semi-final, and went on to dominate the 1970s. Everton sunk to mid-table. Heighway's goal set up more than just an exciting victory over the old enemy.

Teams: *Liverpool:* Clemence, Lawler, Lindsay, Smith, Lloyd, Hughes, Hall, McLaughlin (Boersma), Heighway, Toshack, Ross.
Everton: Rankin, Wright, Newton H, Kendall (Newton K), Labone, Harvey, Whittle, Ball, Royle, Hurst, Morrissey.

John Toshack, in one of his first games for Liverpool, heads the equalizer against Everton in 1970, a match which marked Liverpool's resurgence.

FA Cup Final 1974

Liverpool 3 Newcastle United 0

The FA Cup Final of 1974 promised a great match in prospect. Liverpool were enjoying the third of nine seasons where they never finished lower than the first three in the Championship. At the time Liverpool and Leeds were the strongest sides in the country. But Newcastle United, an inconsistent mid-table side, were not unworthy opponents. They had Alan Kennedy and Terry McDermott, later to be Liverpool stars, Bobby Moncur, an inspiring captain, Terry Hibbitt, a mid-field player of brilliance, and twin strikers, Malcolm Macdonald and John Tudor, who scored breathtaking goals. The charismatic 'Supermac', in particular, had promised to find the net.

Seven of the Liverpool players had been at Wembley in 1971, when they had taken the lead in extra time against Arsenal, only to have the Cup snatched away by two late goals. They were determined there should be no mistakes this time.

For 20 minutes or so Newcastle were sprightly, with Hibbitt worrying the Liverpool defence without managing to tee up a chance for Macdonald or Tudor, the heavy artillery. With Kevin Keegan and Steve Heighway busy but frustrated at the other end, the first half ended with no score and all to play for. But Hibbitt had wrenched his knee in the 40th minute, and he and McDermott faded in the second half, as the Liverpool machine began to move forward irresistibly.

Keegan scores and Newcastle are humiliated 3-0 at Wembley.

98

Soon after half-time Keegan set up what looked like a good goal for Alec Lindsay – it was ruled fractionally offside. There were no doubts in the 58th minute when Keegan scored a brilliant goal, checking Tommy Smith's hard cross and in the fraction of time created volleying home, although two defenders were in attendance. The match was virtually sealed in the 75th minute when Heighway scored his second Cup Final goal (he had scored in 1971) by hitting home Toshack's back-header.

Newcastle, at this stage, were so out of the game that their first corner did not come until the 72nd minute. Liverpool's defence, superbly marshalled by Phil Thompson, had snuffed out Macdonald and Tudor. Macdonald got his first clear opportunity in the 77th minute – it went wide.

Liverpool's superiority was confirmed by the manner of the third goal in the 88th minute. A dozen passes put Smith clear on the right by-line. His low cross found Keegan with so much room that he almost over-ran the ball, but he reached back to tuck it in and complete a masterful personal performance.

The following season Liverpool won the Charity Shield on penalties from Leeds after a brawling match and Bill Shankly handed over to Bob Paisley – in the Cup Final of 1974 he had brought his Liverpool side close to perfection.

Teams: *Liverpool:* Clemence, Smith, Thompson, Hughes, Lindsay, Hall, Callaghan, Cormack, Keegan, Toshack, Heighway.
Newcastle United: McFaul, Clark, Howard, Moncur, Kennedy, Smith (Gibb), McDermott, Cassidy, Macdonald, Tudor, Hibbitt.

European Cup Final, 1977

Liverpool 3 Borussia Moenchengladbach 1

In 1976-77 Liverpool were embarking on their thirteenth successive season in European football. The UEFA Cup had been won twice, the final of the Cup Winners Cup had been lost, but the record in the major competition, the European Cup, was disappointing. After the semi-final appearance in 1964-65, they had got no further than the second round in two subsequent efforts. By 1977 the Kop wanted a win to set the seal on Liverpool's greatness.

Liverpool sought an 'impossible' treble that season. The League Championship was safely gathered in. But four days before the European Cup Final, the FA Cup Final was lost, Manchester United cashing in on a little good fortune to win 2-1. The side had to pick itself up for Rome, and the clash with German Champions Borussia Moenchengladbach.

They did their work well. Always looking dangerous, Liverpool struck in the 27th minute. Ian Callaghan fed Steve Heighway and moved outside him as Heighway cut in on one of his penetrating runs. As Kevin Keegan moved left, taking Berti Vogts with him, Terry McDermott sped towards the area in the inside-right position. Heighway's diagonal pass was perfectly weighted into his path, and McDermott stroked it first time into the far corner for a superb goal and a well-deserved half-time lead.

Tommy Smith heads powerfully and the ball rockets into the Borussia net to give the Reds the lead.

Six minutes after the interval, Phil Neal and Jimmy Case muddled and Case passed straight to Allan Simonsen, the brilliant Danish winger, who moved forward and scored with a tremendous cross-shot. Five minutes later Uli Stielike was thwarted by a brilliant save by Clemence as he dashed from his line, and it looked like the Cup Final over again, with Liverpool failing to convert steady pressure into goals.

The 65th minute settled it. Heighway took a corner on the left, a red-shirted player leapt forward and smacked the ball home with an unstoppable header. To everybody's surprise it turned out to be Tommy Smith, playing because of injury to Phil Thompson, in what he announced as his last match (he later changed his mind).

Liverpool were now on top, and when Keegan, who played brilliantly throughout, went dashing through the middle with seven minutes left to be tripped by Berti Vogts, Phil Neal made no mistake with the penalty. Emlyn Hughes and his men were soon showing the trophy to the 57,000 crowd, nearly half of whom had come from Liverpool. It was the best final for years, and the last, until 1984, to produce more than one goal.

Teams: *Liverpool:* Clemence, Neal, Jones, Smith, Kennedy, Hughes, Keegan, Case, Heighway, Callaghan, McDermott.
Borussia Moenchengladbach: Kneib, Vogts, Klinkhammer, Wittkampf, Bonhof, Wohlers (Hannes), Simonsen, Wimmer (Kulik), Stielike, Schaffer, Heynckes.

Following pages *Emlyn Hughes, the skipper, takes his hat off to the crowd in Rome (many of whom came from Liverpool) after the first European Cup win.*

European Cup Final 1978

Liverpool 1 Bruges 0

When Liverpool reached the European Cup Final in 1978 as Champions, and the final was scheduled for Wembley, there seemed little doubt that the Reds would win again. Their opponents were Bruges, from Belgium, a side which included internationals from Denmark and Austria as well as Belgium. On the way to the Final they had disposed of Atletico Madrid and Juventus, so were clearly not going to be a pushover, but few expected Liverpool to lose.

Liverpool had five changes from the side which had won in Rome, the main one being that Keegan had gone to Germany, to be replaced by Kenny Dalglish. It was Dalglish who was to provide the only memorable moment in a match which was to set an example in cautious play that subsequent European Cup Finals copied.

Bruges were the offenders, showing no inclination to attack at all. Perhaps they thought that if they kept a clean sheet, they might win by a Liverpool mistake. Emlyn Hughes, the captain, went further – he thought they might be hoping to win on a penalty shoot-out. Bruges blamed their poor display on the absence through injury of two of their best players, and no doubt they were aggrieved at what they considered was a 'home' match for Liverpool.

In fact, Liverpool supporters were annoyed at the allocation of tickets to the club – the Wembley final proved more difficult to attend than that in Rome. Those who did get in saw Liverpool attack for an hour, without showing signs of breaking down the massed Belgian defence. When they did manage to get in a shot the Danish international goalkeeper, Birger Jensen, dealt with everything competently.

In the 65th minute came the decisive moment of magic for Liverpool – a goal of real flair for Dalglish. Graeme Souness, Liverpool's other main signing of the season, put Dalglish through on the right side of the area. Dalglish reached the corner of the six-yard box with a defender a pace behind and the goalkeeper advancing rapidly. Dalglish waited for Jensen to dive, and as he spread himself at Dalglish's feet, coolly chipped the ball over his body just inside the far post.

That was effectively the end of the match. Bruges could find no attacking inspiration whatever to help stage a comeback, and with no alarms Liverpool were soon parading the European Cup again – the first British side to win it twice.

Teams: *Liverpool:* Clemence, Neal, Hughes, Thompson, Kennedy R, Hansen, Dalglish, Case (Heighway), Fairclough, McDermott, Souness.
Bruges: Jensen, Bastijns, Maes (Volder), Krieger, Leekens, Cools, De Cubber, Vandereycken, Simoen, Ku (Sanders), Sorensen.

Opposite *Dalglish chips the keeper, and players, linesman and crowd watch the ball on its way into the net.*

European Cup Final 1981

Liverpool 1 Real Madrid 0

Both teams in Paris for the 1981 European Cup Final badly wanted to win. Real, who won the first five competitions, had not won since their record sixth win in 1966. Liverpool had won twice, and wanted to join those clubs, Bayern Munich and Ajax Amsterdam as well as Real Madrid, who had won the Cup three times.

Maybe the importance of winning inhibited both teams. Certainly each side played from the start as if their minds were on a 1-0 victory (the result of the previous three Finals). Gone were the days when Real could joyously win the final 7-3, as they did in 1960, or lose excitingly by 5-3, as they did two years later. In the end, it was Real Madrid who produced slightly more flair, Liverpool who kept plugging away with more consistency.

The first half was marked by a number of hard tackles. The few chances that came to each side were spoiled by hasty and poor shooting. Ray Kennedy was booked for a foul on the goalkeeper during a fierce mêlée in the goalmouth, Clemence caught Santillana's header under the bar and Agustin saved a shot from Souness at the second attempt.

Juanito and Laurie Cunningham, the England international playing in Spain, produced the best football of the first half, and five minutes after half-time Real created the best chance of the match so far when Camacho ran

The Real Madrid goalkeeper narrows the angle but Alan Kennedy blasts the ball past him for the winner.

on to a clever lob over the Liverpool defence. As Clemence advanced he neatly chipped the ball over the keeper, but just over the bar.

Uli Stielike, playing against Liverpool for the second time in a European Cup Final, joined Kennedy in the referee's book, and Santillana twice came close to the vital touch. But it was the Liverpool machine, getting stronger as Real faded, which pressed forward.

Alan Kennedy found Cunningham, who had returned after six month's injury, needed less attention as the match wore on, and in the 82nd minute he took on his chest a Ray Kennedy throw-in well in Real's half and swept on into the area, brushing aside a weak tackle from Cortes. The angle was narrow and Agustin moved to cut out a cross, but Kennedy fired a savage shot between him and the near post into the roof of the net. Madrid attacked, but nearly conceded another goal in the remaining minutes as Agustin saved brilliantly at close range from Souness. Phil Thompson collected the Cup, Hughes having moved on to Wolves, and Bob Paisley became the first manager to win three European Cups. And Liverpool had become the fourth team to register a third win since the competition was started.

Teams: *Liverpool:* Clemence, Neal, Thompson, Hansen, Kennedy A, Lee, McDermott, Souness, Kennedy R, Dalglish (Case), Johnson.
Real Madrid: Agustin, Garcia Cortes (Pineda), Garcia Navajas, Sabido, Del Bosque, Angel, Camacho, Stielike, Juanito, Santillana, Cunningham.

Football League Milk Cup Final 1982

Liverpool 3 Tottenham Hotspur 1

The Football League Milk Cup Final at Wembley in 1982 provided another of those familiar occasions when Liverpool refused to give up, kept pressing remorselessly, struck when all seemed lost and eventually emerged as winners so comfortable that it seemed impossible that a few minutes earlier they had been on the brink of defeat.

Liverpool began with assurance, but a chapter of accidents plus opportunism by Steve Archibald caused them to fall behind in the 11th minute. Archibald beat Thompson and Lawrenson to a Hoddle cross, Thompson's hurried attempt at a clearance hit Archibald's legs, and as Grobbelaar came out Archibald was the nimblest of all to slide the ball home.

Liverpool pressed, but Ray Clemence, now having a second lease of life with Spurs, saved easily from Sammy Lee and Ian Rush miskicked with a clear chance.

In the second half Liverpool constantly pressed forward, but Spurs, prompted by neat play by Ardiles and Hazard, looked to be just as dangerous in breakaways. Hazard tested Grobbelaar, who also had to dive at Crooks' feet to make a save. Meanwhile, despite their intense pressure,

Ron Whelan scores against old Liverpool favourite Ray Clemence, and Liverpool are on the way to their second League Cup success.

Liverpool looked to be running out of scoring ideas, with Clemence dealing competently with some long shots. Five minutes before the end of normal time Archibald could have sealed the match for Spurs when he won the ball in a tussle with Grobbelaar, but Souness managed to clear the ball off the goal line.

With three minutes to go weary Spurs made their first mistake. A cross from Johnson on the right was allowed to reach Ronnie Whelan, who drove the ball home just inside the far post.

In extra time, there was only one likely winning team, although it was five minutes into the second period before Liverpool clinched it. Ardiles, who had run everywhere, uncharacteristically gave the ball to Rush, who found Dalglish, and Ronnie Whelan moved in to accept the pass and score. The sun came out, the Reds rolled on, and just before the end Johnson and Rush went through and Rush made the score 3-1 – strange to think that Spurs had led for an hour and a quarter and had been within three minutes of winning. But Liverpool play for the whole 90 minutes – plus 30 more if necessary.

Teams: *Liverpool:* Grobbelaar, Neal, Kennedy A, Thompson, Whelan, Lawrenson, Dalglish, Lee, Rush, McDermott (Johnson), Souness.
Tottenham Hotspur: Clemence, Hughton, Miller, Price, Hazard (Villa), Perryman, Ardiles, Archibald, Galvin, Hoddle, Crooks.

Football League Milk Cup Final 1984

Liverpool 0 Everton 0 (*after extra time*) **Liverpool 1 Everton 0**

On Sunday, 25 March 1984, Wembley staged the first all-Merseyside final. Liverpool, the leading team in the country for a decade, and once more at the head of the First Division race, were playing Everton, for just as long in comparative decline. The Football League Milk Cup was the prize. At any time in the previous few seasons, the result would have been easy to forecast, but in the weeks leading to the Final, Everton had begun a revival. They were in the semi-finals of the FA Challenge Cup (they went on to win it), and had drawn 1-1 with Liverpool in the League three weeks earlier. Their supporters considered they had a chance, and the match provoked much comment and speculation as the date approached. Thousands of supporters of both sides made the trip south.

The match began at a furious pace in the rain, and the confidence of Everton fans seemed not unplaced as the blue shirts tore into Liverpool. The Reds seemed bemused. After eight minutes Heath won a 50-50 ball from Grobbelaar, and, sitting on the ground, hooked it towards an empty net. Hansen, rushing in, intercepted the bouncing ball with what to the crowd appeared to be his thigh and hand. The penalty was not awarded. Nothing daunted, Everton continued to play at express speed for an hour, and most of the best chances fell to them in an exciting match.

In the last half hour Liverpool's more measured play began to produce the better opportunities, and Rush managed to put a bobbling ball over the bar from five yards out. Sheedy was injured for Everton and Harper was substituted, but Everton made the final effort of ordinary time, Sharp shooting wide with two minutes left.

Craig Johnston was replaced by Michael Robinson for extra time. After four minutes Rush met a centre with a superb volley, but Southall turned it aside. Then Sharp and Heath caused a mix-up in the Liverpool defence which ended with Neal luckily deflecting the ball to Grobbelaar. At the end both sets of supporters chanted 'Merseyside, Merseyside' and the teams were presented to the Queen Mother. It had been a satisfying game, and nobody (if the penalty incident is discounted) could feel disappointed.

For the replay at Maine Road the following Wednesday, Harper this time began the match for Everton, while Johnston, who had walked off alone in obvious dejection at Wembley, again lined up for Liverpool.

Everton began as in the first encounter, with passion, and gave better than they received, Harper shooting wildly when well placed, and Grobbelaar saving well from Reid. Then, in the 22nd minute, Souness settled it for Liverpool. A move involving him, Neal and Dalglish saw him receive the ball on the edge of the area. As he turned, it appeared he had few options, but he found one: he swung his left foot and the ball beat Southall's late dive to go in near the post.

The match continued at top speed, and both sides might have scored another goal, but neither could, and Liverpool became the first side in English football to win the same major trophy four years in succession.

Teams: *Liverpool:* Grobbelaar, Neal, Kennedy A, Lawrenson, Whelan, Hansen, Dalglish, Lee, Rush, Johnston (Robinson sub in first match), Souness.
Everton: Southall, Stevens, Bailey, Ratcliffe, Mountfield, Reid, Irvine, Heath, Sharp, Richardson, Sheedy (Harper sub in first match and replacement in second).

Preceding pages *Everton
pressed hard in the 1984 Milk
Cup Final, but Bruce Grobbelaar
was equal to them in the air or on
the ground.*

European Cup Final 1984

Liverpool 1 AS Roma 1 *(after extra time)*
Liverpool won 4-2 on penalties

Liverpool, having played superbly to reach the Final of the European Cup
on 30 May 1984, faced just about the most difficult task any side could in a
final. Their opponents were AS Roma, and by a cruel twist of fate the
venue, decided months before, was the Stadio Olimpico in Rome. The local
citizens were not disposed to spurn this gift. The Italian capital was
bedecked with bunting in the colours of the home team, red and gold, and
the Roman holiday to celebrate the win began before the match started.

Below *The teams take the field
among flags, fireworks, smoke
and noise.*

The Liverpool side were in no mood to offer themselves for slaughter,
however, and from the kick-off their experience, calm and composure were
evident as they stroked the ball around at a leisurely pace. Roma would not

win by default. The World Cup heroes, Conti and Graziani, and the brilliant Brazilians, Falcao and Cerezo, would have to battle.

In the 15th minute, Liverpool scored a lucky goal. A deep centre from Johnston caused the Roma goalkeeper to backpedal to the edge of the six-yard box. As he jumped to catch the ball, Whelan challenged behind him. Tancredi dropped the ball. The referee, surprisingly, allowed play to continue. Bonetti and Nappi were at hand to clear – one tried to head the ball past the post, the other to help it on its way by blasting it towards the corner flag. Unfortunately it hit Tancredi, who was attempting to scramble up, on the head, and rebounded to the feet of Phil Neal. He prodded it into the empty net.

Liverpool appeared completely in control until two minutes before half-time. Conti then got the ball to the by-line on the left, but his centre was blocked. He reached the rebound and centred with his right foot, and Pruzzo flicked a beautiful looping header over Grobbelaar into the far corner to equalize.

Roma dominated the first 20 minutes of the second half, then Liverpool gradually took command again. Further goals would not come, although a typical penalty area pass from Dalglish almost put in Nicol, who had replaced Johnston with 20 minutes to go. Soon after extra time began, Dalglish himself, whose moments of inspiration had been rare, was taken off and Robinson came on. Although the Reds were comfortably in control, they could not score, and the match reached the stage when penalty kicks would decide.

And what drama the penalty shoot-out brought!

The goal chosen was that before the massed Roma supporters. Liverpool were to take the first penalty. Phil Neal, the only survivor from the first European Cup win in 1977, and the regular spot-kicker, was ready to take it, but Steve Nicol volunteered. Alas, the bravado misfired. Nerves are not conquered so easily. Nicol blazed wildly over, the crowd cheered, and for the first time for two hours it seemed that Roma held the upper hand.

Graziani approached the spot to take Roma's first penalty, but the captain, Di Bartolomei, took the ball from him. With just two paces, he hit it into the net to put Roma ahead. The feeling that this was not Liverpool's day deepened, as the shot was dead straight – had Grobbelaar shut his eyes and stood still it would have hit his chest, but, as goalkeepers do, Bruce anticipated, dived, and dived out of the way. Neal netted for Liverpool, and then Conti, of all people – many experts' choice as the best player in the World Cup Final and outstanding again on this night – casually and feebly put the ball over the bar.

All square again. Souness and Righetti netted: 2-2. Rush, scorer of 49 goals in the season, slotted home his kick. Then Graziani stepped up again for his. Another high one – it grazed the top of the bar and sailed away towards the now silent Roma hordes. It was now 3-2, and if Alan Kennedy scored his penalty, that would be that. He said later: 'I was really confident. I took a penalty at training on Monday and put it in the same spot. Just like that'.

For the second time Kennedy had put the ball in the net to decide a European Cup Final for Liverpool. It was their fourth win. There was just Real Madrid's six to overtake now.

Teams: *Liverpool:* Grobbelaar, Neal, Kennedy A, Lawrenson, Whelan, Hansen, Dalglish (Robinson), Lee, Rush, Johnston (Nicol), Souness.
Roma: Tancredi, Nappi, Bonetti, Righetti, Nela, Falcao, Di Bartolomei, Cerezo (Strukelj), Conti, Pruzzo (Chierico), Graziani.

FA Cup Final 1986

Liverpool 3 Everton 1

Despite challenges from Manchester United, Chelsea and West Ham, Liverpool and Everton had proved themselves the two best sides in the country in 1985-86. The Wembley encounter was between the first and second in the League, the Champions of last year against the newly-crowned Champions of this.

It was two years since the first Merseyside final at Wembley, but this was a grander occasion – the first FA Cup Final between the two clubs. Moreover, Liverpool, the Champions, were seeking to emulate Preston North End, Aston Villa, Tottenham Hotspur and Arsenal, and become the fifth side to achieve the classic League and Cup Double.

Kenny Dalglish, in his first season as player-manager, had shuffled his players so often during the season (sometimes because of injury) that it was difficult to predict his Final side. Would he employ a sweeper, and if so would it be Lawrenson or Molby? Would Gillespie play in defence, or McMahon or MacDonald in midfield? Could Lee or Wark or Walsh find a place? Dalglish's final decision (there was a story that his wife, Marina, helped him pick the team) was to play without a sweeper, and Kevin MacDonald was the lucky player chosen for the final midfield spot.

MacDonald was the first player to threaten a goal, but it was Everton who gradually assumed control of the game. Liverpool played with a back four and a packed midfield, but it was the Everton midfield, particularly the industrious Bracewell, who most determined the direction of the play.

In the 20th minute came the most controversial incident of the game. In an Everton attack an angled centre for Stevens appeared to be nicely flighted for Sharp to head in from around six yards. But even as the leaping Sharp shaped to make contact, Nicol tore in from behind with a lunging tackle, the effect of which was to knock Sharp completely off balance. Referee Alan Robinson, who had smiled on Liverpool when refusing Everton a penalty in the Milk Cup Final, remained consistent and refused another, despite Sharp's vehement protests.

The incident was temporarily forgotten nine minutes later, when Reid played a perfectly weighted through ball beyond Lineker and Hansen. Lineker's speed of the mark stole a couple of yards on Hansen, and his left-foot ground shot from near the edge of the area was just hard enough to prevent the advancing and diving Grobbelaar from holding it. Lineker was first to the rebound, and although Grobbelaar rose to dive again at his feet, and once again get his hands on the ball, he could only check its momentum on its way to the net.

Everton were well worth their half-time lead, and began the second half as if they would over-run Liverpool. The Liverpool defence suddenly exhibited the sort of jitters that had given away two own-goals in the Milk Cup semi-final with Queen's Park Rangers. The ball bounced from defender to defender as if the Liverpool penalty area were a pin-table. Hansen looked bewildered and even Lawrenson, who was generally clearing up the mess, gave the ball away. Sheedy almost scored after one lapse, his right-foot shot curling the wrong way and past the post, and again nearly beat Grobbelaar at the foot of his post from a free-kick. Light relief for the impartial was provided by Grobbelaar and Beglin making a mess of giving the ball to each other at the edge of the area – Grobbelaar pushed Beglin in the chest in his anger and embarrassment. It seemed another Everton goal must come.

Then, in the 57th minute, Everton made what by comparison was a harmless error. Stevens attempted a pass from defence along the touchline, but it was easily intercepted by Whelan and transferred to Molby. He slid a diagonal pass into the area and Rush, sprinting past his markers, touched the ball around Mimms and rolled it home.

The following six minutes settled the match. Everton, who in the previous two seasons had become almost as match-hard as Liverpool, did not waver after this unexpected reverse, but pushed forward again. The Liverpool defence made its final mistake. With Grobbelaar advancing to collect a bouncing ball near the corner of the penalty area, Hansen intervened to slice the ball high towards the centre of his own half. It described an inviting arc onto the head of Sharp who powered a long-range header towards the empty goal. It was perfectly executed, but matched by Grobbelaar's dash back and gigantic leap which just managed to push the ball over the bar.

Two minutes later, in the 63rd minute, Rush found Molby on the left. He charged into the area and played a square ball across the face of the goal. Dalglish just missed it, but Johnston was behind him at the far post to sidefoot home.

This goal virtually settled the match. Suddenly Liverpool were getting the ball in midfield, and the defence became secure. Everton took off Stevens and substituted Heath, who had scored vital goals in similar situations during the season. But, although the Everton attack continued to buzz, gaps appeared at the back. Six minutes from the end, Rush was involved in a passing movement out of defence. The ball went from Molby to Whelan in a sweeping move up the left. Whelan's precise cross found Rush, having advanced three-quarters of the length of the pitch up the right, with the composure to control the ball with one touch and hammer it home with another.

The last six minutes were a sort of Liverpool victory parade, during which Rush might have completed a hat-trick, his attempted chip suggesting mercy towards the goalkeeper.

Liverpool had won a match which seemed lost merely by keeping going until they hit the front. It was a summing up in one match of the way they had won the Championship.

It had been a fine match, which despite the occasional error had been characterized by strong, attacking football, a splendid contrast to the negative, boring European Cup Final of a few days earlier. While they won impressively in the end, Liverpool realized that the match hinged on three or four incidents which went their way, and that it could easily have been Everton playing the arrogant, winning football in the end. This did not detract from the victory. They had emerged the better of two fine teams, and their Double triumph crowned a decade of outstanding achievement.

Teams: *Liverpool*: Grobbelaar, Nicol, Beglin, Lawrenson, Whelan, Hansen, Dalglish, Johnston, Rush, Molby, MacDonald.
Everton: Mimms, Stevens (Heath), van den Hauwe, Ratcliffe, Mountfield, Reid, Steven, Lineker, Sharp, Bracewell, Sheedy.

Following pages *Rush scores the third goal in Liverpool's 3–1 defeat of Everton in the 1986 FA Cup final.*

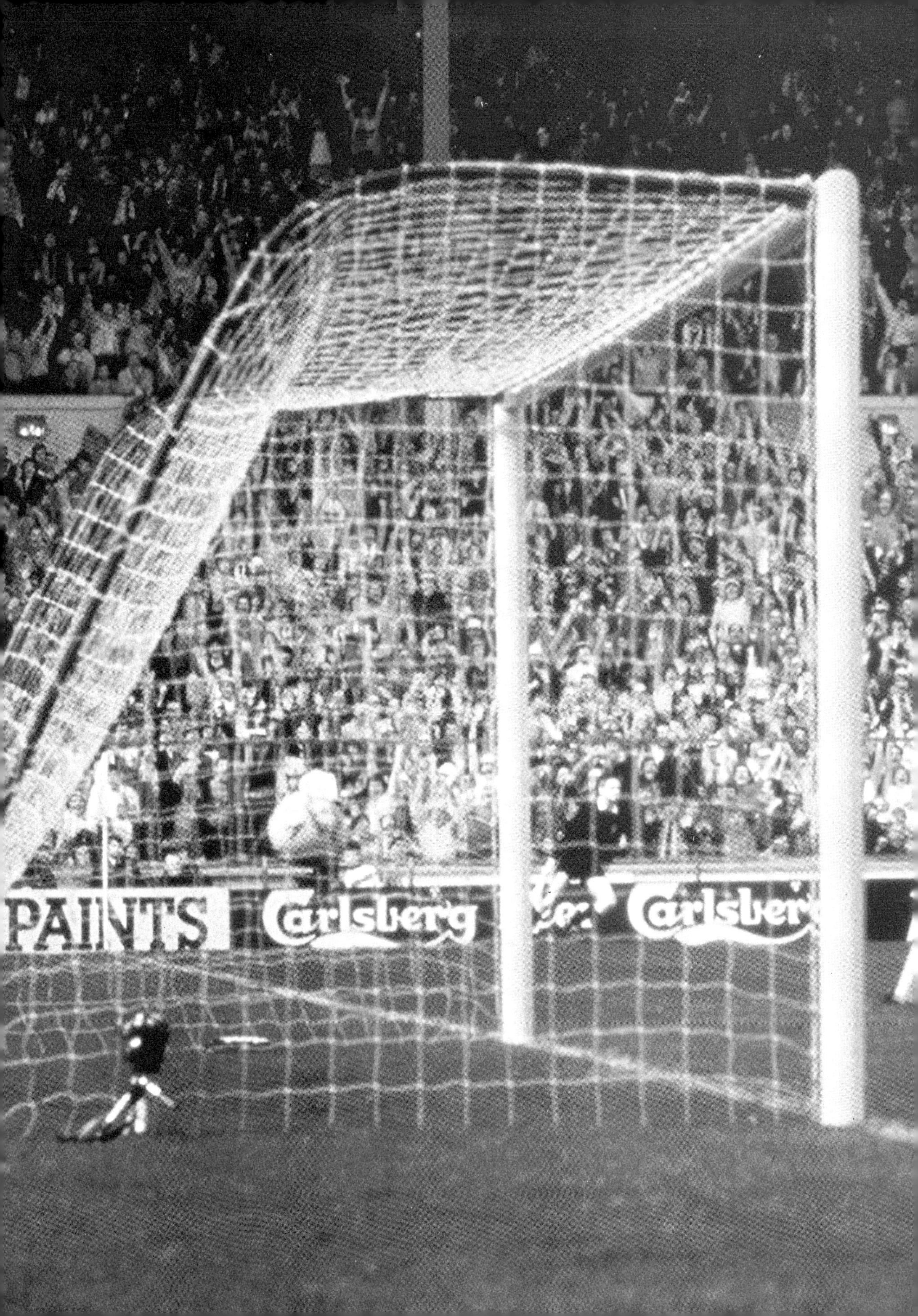
PAINTS
Carlsberg
Carlsberg

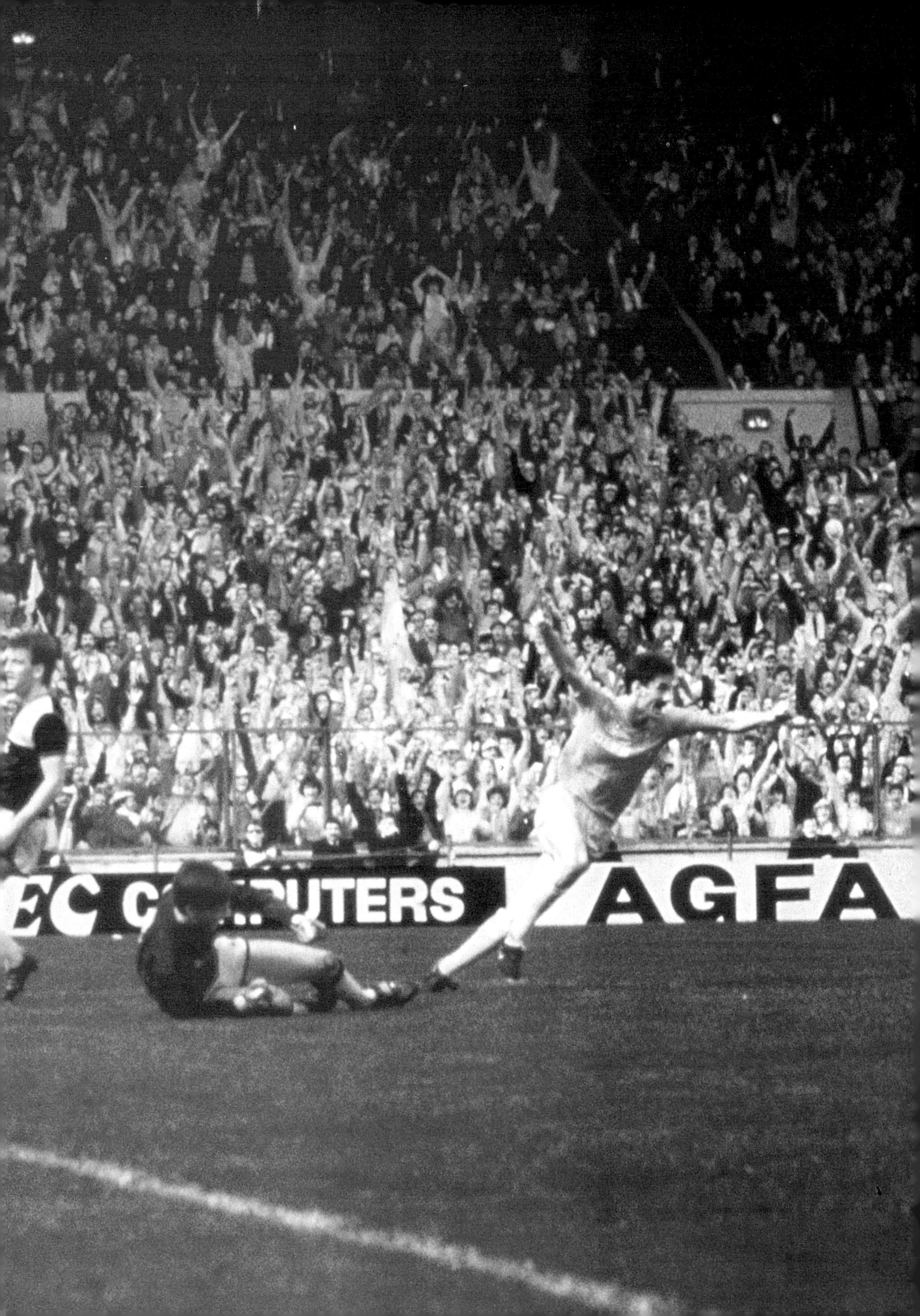
EC C…UTERS
AGFA

Index

Page numbers in *italic* refer to the illustrations